To Kristn

Go Ahead

Joshua Lee Patton's

Go Ahead

Say It Like It Is

R. L. "Duke" Tirschel

To order additional copies of this book, contact:
Xlibris Corporation
1-888-795-4274
www.Xlibris.com
Orders@Xlibris.com
41244

Contents

Preface

Harold Junior Anderson grew up in a two room shack with seven brothers and five sisters in the mountains of North Georgia. He was laughed at for going to school barefoot and he was bullied because he didn't fit in. When forced to quit school he made a living making moonshine and running whiskey, stealing cars and stealing cattle.

When he was a teenager, three men ten years older and twice his size were trying to kill him. The sheriff who killed Harold's cousin, Snake Martin, hired the man who ran the 'stake-out' squad in Atlanta to kill Harold Anderson and his friends.

That was the way Harold Junior Anderson lived before he was run out of Dahlonega.

He stayed away for two years but when he returned he had combat training and military discipline, he had a purpose and direction in life that he acquired in the United States Marine Corps, and what's more, he had a .30-06 caliber World War II sniper rifle with the ammunition and plenty of reason to use it.

The night lights from the Federal Savings and Loan building reflect off the wet pavement of the parking lot. A gust of wind sends a yellow piece of crime-scene tape skidding across the white chalked outline where, moments ago, a bullet riddled body was lying on the ground.

The last spectator shrugs and shakes his head and disappears into the shadows. A siren is fading in the distance as the ambulance carries the dead and the wounded away. Once the search gets underway for the man who is missing and the shooter is taken to jail the only one left at the scene is you.

You shrug too, but you stay and stare into the empty space, dazed by how quickly the quiet returns. The shooting that just took place was not a senseless act but you can't seem to make sense of what you saw.

Actually, there *is* no sense to be made of it; not by what we know so far.

Even the next day's newspaper, *The Times,* in Gainesville, Georgia, didn't make sense of it. The paper said three men awaiting trial for illegal possession of hand grenades and explosives chased down and then attacked a young man and a shooting occurred. They quoted the sheriff saying, *"I watched the shooting from my window but I couldn't go to the scene since I didn't have my shoes on."* And so, while the sheriff looks for his shoes a man is killed, another man is critically wounded, one man ends up missing and the man under attack is arrested at the scene and charged with murder.

The newspaper knew very little about the real story behind this shooting and that's why the newspaper account doesn't make sense. That's because the real story didn't *start* there, and regardless of who killed who, the real story didn't *end* there, either.

This is *the real story* of the 'Dahlonega Square Shootout' in 1975.

Introduction

Harold Anderson placed his World War II sniper rifle on the seat next to him and opened a fresh box of .30-06 caliber ammunition. He kept his eyes on the black Ford that chased him into the parking lot and was blocking his only way out. The three men in the black Ford; Snooks Brackett, Archie Berry, and Doug Walker think they have Harold cornered. But, the truth of the matter is that Harold Junior Anderson has these three men exactly where he wants them.

These three men bullied Harold up until he left Dahlonega to join the Marine Corps two years ago. And now that Harold's back, these men think there's some unfinished business they need to settle. It never did sit right with them that Harold never gave in to them and each time they butt heads, Harold came away with the upper hand. That was embarrassing for them, and now, they would like to settle some old scores.

On the other side of the coin, Harold feels that maybe he hasn't done enough to get the point across to all of them that he's not going to be bullied, especially now that he's older and just finished two years in the Marine Corps.

Less than an hour earlier, Harold was driving though town and was surprised to see that after all this time these same three men were still hanging out on the square When Harold started to pass them they waved him over to the curb and tried to pull him out of his van. Harold decided to face them in a more secluded spot and so he spun around them and sped away.

Harold led them out of town and unwittingly they followed.

Harold wasn't running but it sure looked like it, and that seemed to stir things up. Archie Berry was in the back seat, Doug Walker was riding shotgun and Snooks Brackett was driving and he had the accelerator to the floor. They were like little kids all bent forward at the waist as if by leaning in the direction they were going they could make their car go faster.

Harold wanted to get out of town where no one could see how he planned to take care of business, but before he reached the edge of town, Snooks Brackett's black Ford rammed the back of Harold's van and spun him around in front of the First Federal Savings and Loan building.

It was Sunday so the lot was empty. It was getting dark and no one else was around and so Harold smiled as Snooks Brackett's car followed him into the parking lot and blocked the only way out. Harold's old van sat at one end of the lot and the old black Ford at the other. They were facing each other with engines running and the beams of their headlights crossed each other in the space of the empty lot between them.

Everyone stayed in their cars.

Snooks Brackett, Archie Berry, and Doug Walker were taking their time 'strapping up' for the battle. Harold pulled out a long .30-06 caliber cartridge with its pointed metal jacket and felt the weight of it in the palm of his hand before placing it in the breech of his rifle. But then, with one hand on the bolt action lever, he froze. He sat perfectly still and focused his attention on Brackett's car as the passenger's side door swung open.

The door stood open but no one got out. Several seconds passed before Harold let loose the breath he held and slid the bolt on his rifle home. He put the rest of the cartridges in his jacket pocket and placed his rifle on the seat next to him. As Harold waited he recalled bits and pieces of the last encounter he had with each one of these men. It interested him to note that each time he faced any of them in the past there was always someone with a shotgun and there was always a message that, in effect, said . . . *this is not the time.*

He recalled his run-in with his cousin Doug Walker who was 6'11" 340 lbs.

"He was on his knees after I kicked him in the nuts. I was pounding his head in but I had to stop when JC showed up and blew the roof off the all-night station with his two automatic shotguns. Then JC hollered over to me, 'Come on little buddy . . . let's get out of here, *this is not the time'.*"

Archie Berry was 6'5" 250 lbs.

"He pulled me over one night because I kicked Doug Walker's ass and that embarrassed his bully friends because I was only 5'9" and only weighed a buck 35, a buck 40 at the most. I put my shotgun on Archie Berry and told him to choose whether he wanted to fight or get his head blown off. He said he'd leave; because, *this is not the time.*

Snooks Brackett was 6'3" 240 lbs and the meanest of the bunch.

"One night Snooks swung at me, and I ducked and hit him one time right between the eyes and knocked him flat of his ass, and before I could even get my senses, this bitch turned me a flip right in the middle of the parking lot.

He said, 'Yeah, get up now, mother fucker.'

I got up and ran to my car, pulled out my shotgun and said, 'Motherfucker, it's your night tonight' and I pulled the hammer back.

One of my big ass buddies grabbed my gun and said, 'No, Harold; *this is not the time'.*"

That was Harold's last encounter with each one of these men and now he's facing all of them at the same time. Harold's choice is being made for him, because . . . *this **is** the time.* This must be the time that people mean when they talk about being *in the moment.*

When Doug Walker jumped out of Brackett's car, Harold drew in a deep breath and let it out slow. A bead of sweat ran down the side of his neck as he slid back the bolt on his rifle and seeing the .30-06 caliber round in the breech he gave one quick nod of his head and slid the bolt back home.

Harold squint his eyes and cocked his head slightly to one side as he saw everything moving in slow motion. He saw Archie Berry in the back seat aiming a pistol through the back side window. Snooks Brackett pulled out his nickel plated .38 and started to climb out from behind the driver's side.

Doug Walker had already crossed the parking lot and was making his way around the side of Harold's car. Harold ran his hands down the pant legs of his fatigues to wipe the sweat from his palms, and then grabbing his rifle, he got out of the car and stepped up to face *the moment.*

One

Grandmother's House

In the foothills of the Blue Ridge Mountains, a wide dirt road runs between the sycamore and purple ash trees that line Wimpy Mill road in Dahlonega, Georgia. A quarter mile away a trail of dust is being kicked up by an old pick up truck that's speeding towards us. It swerves all the way to one side of the road and then suddenly cuts back to the other side, and it does this repeatedly as it's coming towards us. Running in front of the car is a figure you don't see at first because it is so small. But as the car gets closer you can see the figure is a small boy.

Harold Junior Anderson is six years old. He lives down the road from his parent's farm with his Grandmother, Mary Anderson. Harold has made a habit of running away from his Grandmother's house and sneaking back home in hopes that his parents will let him stay.

And if it was up to his mother, Janelle, he *would* be able to stay.

Janelle is a small lady with a big heart. She is just as warm and loving to her seven boys and five girls as her husband Henry Anderson is stern. Whenever she sees that Harold has come back she would stop whatever work she's doing and call to him, "Why, Junior Anderson, you little rascal. Come on give me a hug."

Harold cautiously looked towards the house and then towards the barn, "Is daddy . . . ?"

Janelle held her arms out, "No . . . your daddy went to town."

Harold put his arms around his mother's neck and squeezed.

Janelle held him out at arms length, "Let me see you . . . wow, look at those muscles."

Harold said proudly, "I've been hauling the water from the well every day . . ." and then Harold's eyes suddenly opened wide. The sound of his daddy's truck was heard coming up the road.

Janelle turned Harold around by his shoulders, gave him a little shove of his back side and said, "Go on, Junior . . . quick, run . . . get on back to Mary's."

Harold thought his mother was the kindest most wonderful person in the world and it was always worth sneaking home just to spend a minute with her. When Henry Anderson wouldn't be back for a long while she didn't rush to send Harold back. She would let him help her hang out the laundry or do some chore that was needed. He knew he wasn't that much help and that his mother just wanted him around. That feeling of being wanted felt good.

On the other hand, when his daddy caught him coming back to the house he gave Harold a whipping and sent him back to his grandmother's. He doesn't *always* chase Harold back with the truck, but on this particular day, his father was drunk and he wasn't really chasing him back to Mary's house, he was, literally, going to try to run him down. And so, Harold started running as hard as he could because he knew that when his daddy was drunk he could run him over and not even remember it the next day.

Henry Anderson was a lean, raw boned-as-a bull kind of person. He was 5'9" and weighed 170 pounds and was a hard working man. He, and his wife Janelle, had all those mouths to feed and for the most part he was a good man. As a matter of fact, Henry Anderson was the kindest and the nicest person you would ever want to meet; when he was sober.

But, when he was drunk he was a monster.

As soon as Harold reached his Grandmother's house he ran to the back where his father couldn't get to him, and so, Henry settled for yelling at Harold, "You run off one more time and I will . . .

for-sure . . . run your ass over."

Harold was next to the youngest boy and too young for the farm work, but he was able to do the work his Grandmother needed and so Harold's father sent him to live with her . . . and Harold hated it.

Harold's Grandmother, Mary Anderson, was part Cherokee Indian with long snow-white hair that almost reached the ground. She was about five foot tall, had a slender build and looked frail, but she wasn't. She was mean as Hell and just as tough.

Harold lived with her when he was six years old and every day she made him carry water from the well that was a hundred yards back in the woods. He carried two buckets almost as big as him, one in each hand. He carried all the water for whatever was needed; and he did that every day. Water was needed for clothes to be washed, for the cooking, and for the baths. It would take dozens of trips, and he was not to spill one drop or his Grandmother would whip him.

Harold knew he would be needed back to work at the farm as soon as he was strong enough to do the work, and that's why he went home so often. He wanted to see when he would be needed and when he could stay home. Most of the time he didn't get caught sneaking back. On one of those days, that his daddy was gone, Harold came back home and was helping his mother with some fire wood.

Janelle said, "You know Harold, your cousins take up a lot of room and they're leaving. They're going to North Carolina."

"When?"

"Any day, now . . . Eugene said he might be moving off soon, too."

"Who's going to help daddy with the still?"

"Monroe is going to do that."

"Then who's going to help daddy at the farmers market?"

"Oh, I don't know, darling . . . I guess either George or David."

"What about the farming? There's nothing I can't do around the farm."

Janelle smiled, "I know that, darling . . . but I bet . . . well, I better leave it up to your daddy to say when . . . but, it won't be long."

Carrying those buckets of water made Harold strong and Henry was needing another pair of hands around the farm, and school was starting, too. It was time for Harold to move back home and help with the work on the farm and get ready to go to school. He started out feeding the chickens, cleaning the barn, milking the cows, and he helped load his daddy's truck when they carried the produce to the farmers market in Forest Park. Harold was always the first one working and the last one to stop, and he was always quiet about it. He never complained about the work he was told to do, he just did it.

When Harold was a little older he carried hundred pound sacks of sugar from one end of the chicken house to the other for his father's still, and when he finished with that he helped load the one gallon jugs of liquor on the truck so his dad and Monroe could take it to town and sell it. There was something about working hard that made Harold feel closer to his dad. It was special for Harold to be able to work around his father. No one work as hard and long as his father did. His dad taught him how to shoe a horse, milk a cow, and mend a fence, and he even taught him how to make moonshine.

Henry Anderson would show Harold, just once, the proper way something was to be done and Harold knew to do it right from then on. His father taught Harold that he needed to put his heart into everything he did, or else, not do it at all. He was taught that it was one's hard work that was the key to getting ahead.

But Harold's father emphasized that he needed to work hard in school, too. Harold's older brothers may have dropped out of school but Mr. Anderson wanted things to be different for Harold. He wanted Harold to stay in school because Henry Anderson felt for sure, that out of all the other boys, Harold would be the one to make something of him self.

Two

Beginning School

Henry Anderson's house was a two room shack with no running water or bathroom. The toilets were the two Johnny houses out by the barn. The light came through the cracks in the walls in the day time and at night you could count the chickens running under the house through the cracks in the floor. The wood stove was in the big room where all the kids slept and Harold's mom and dad, Janelle and Henry, slept in the small room.

One night there was a noise in the yard that woke Henry. His eyes popped open but he stayed perfectly still and without taking his head off the pillow he strained to listen, and there it was, he heard it again. It was a familiar sound of something scratching on wood out by the chicken house. The pit bull at the foot of the bed began to growl and Henry whispered, "Whoa there . . . don't give us a way, boy." When he heard the scratching sound again he slowly inched his way out of bed, went to the door leading into the big room and whispered through the half opened door, "Monroe, get up . . . but be quiet."

Monroe was a lean boy with dark hair and was a lot like his father, quiet and gentle, and mannerly, too. But when he is drunk he gets just as mean as his father does when his father gets drunk. Henry Anderson called on Monroe to do most everything.

"Monroe," Henry whispered louder this time, "Get your .22 . . . we're going to get that damn fox this time . . . I heard him . . . he's around behind the chicken house." Henry warmed his hands on the pot belly stove and waited impatiently for Monroe to get his pants on, "You don't need shoes . . . c'mon, now . . . hurry."

Henry and Monroe went around the side of the house and started across the yard just as a dark red blur ran out of the chicken house. The fox didn't have time to take any of the hens but Monroe missed getting a shot at him, too. Frustrated, Henry threw a rock into the trees in the direction the fox ran, "Aw, shit, damn it to hell, anyway."

Monroe jumped, "Damn, he surprised me . . . that sucker was fast."

"Let it go . . . grab some wood before coming in . . . and latch that damn door to the chicken house . . . who keeps leaving it open, anyway?" Henry went back to bed while Monroe grabbed a couple chunks of wood and brought them in to put on the fire.

Harold sat up in the corner, "Didn't get 'em . . . did ya?"

"Go back to sleep, Harold."

Harold got up and came over to the fire, "Why didn't you shoot, Roe?"

"It was just a fox . . . he didn't get anything. Now, go on. Get back to sleep."

Harold went back to his bedroll in the corner, pulled up his wooly blanket and whispered, "Hey Roe, did daddy say anything about me?"

Monroe's tone was mean, "Boy, what would daddy have anything about you to say?"

"If he needed me tomorrow or if I had to go to that stupid school, that's all."

"He don't give a flip what you do . . . get the barn cleaned out . . . and another load of sugar's coming in so don't be going off anywhere till he says you can."

Monroe stirred the fire and the yellowish light from the stove spread out and fell on a half dozen bed rolls scattered around the room. When the flames shrunk back into the stove the light was drawn in with it and out of the darkness a small inquisitive voice asked, "Did he say I have to go to school tomorrow?"

"Go to sleep Harold."

To Harold, there was nothing out of the ordinary about the way he lived. It wasn't odd to him that he didn't have a pair of shoes or that he didn't have any clothes that fit. In this respect, he was different than the other kids in school. But, he was different at home, too. Because, unlike his brothers, Harold wanted to learn, he wanted to be smart.

Harold was curious about everything and he asked a lot of questions. He liked knowing how things worked and how they got to be the way they were. From the first day Harold watched Monroe get on the bus to go to school he couldn't wait until he was old enough to do the same.

When that day came Harold was just as excited as any other kid going to school for the first time. He stood barefoot at the side of the road waiting for the school bus to come. When Harold got on the bus his brother Monroe pushed right past him. He acted as though he didn't even know Harold. He ignored him and sat with some of the older kids. All the kids on the bus stopped what they were doing and stared at Harold as he stood in the aisle at the front of the bus. The bus was crowded and so when Harold came to a row that had an empty aisle seat, the kid by the window moved over and sat in it and said, "This seat's taken" and pointed Harold to the back of the bus. He just figured that's the way it was done and so he always took his seat, by himself, in the back of the bus.

Harold stuck out in everything he said and in everything he did, and the other kids laughed at him because of it. Harold referred to the other kids as rich kids. They weren't rich. They were just kids who wore shoes, had clothes that fit and enjoyed letting Harold know that he was poor. But, most of all, they wanted Harold to know that he didn't fit in.

He was too little to be fighting the older kids who picked on him, but he had to fight them anyway. He would be punching and kicking and crying all the while they were beating the crap out of him. One day when Harold was getting beat by a couple boys he begged his older brother, Eugene, to help him out. But Eugene had no back bone as far as fighting goes, and so he told Harold, "Well you going to have to grow up and be a man one of these days. You might as well take your whipping or learn how to whip them." And so Harold took his whipping and Eugene just sat back and stayed out of it.

Before long, Harold stayed to himself and quit asking questions. It wasn't that he didn't want to know the answer to the questions that he had . . . it just wasn't worth everyone laughing at him for asking. Harold didn't just quit asking questions, he quit being curious altogether, about anything they tried to teach him at school.

It seemed impossible for him to fit in anywhere.

Three

Family at Home

It was dinner time.

All the boys were either working in the barn or playing in the yard. The girls were helping their mother inside. Shirley and Sue were setting the table when Janelle came out of her room carrying Sylvia. Janelle called for Mildred who was still in the other room, "Millie baby, go get the boys . . . tell them daddy won't be home for supper tonight . . . and to come on."

Mildred ran out the door yelling, "Sonny . . . Harold . . . David . . . Eugene . . ."

Janelle yelled out to Mildred, "Millie . . . Eugene's with your daddy . . . he won't be home tonight, either . . . and oh yes . . . get Ruby . . . I haven't seen her all afternoon . . . she's probably playing with the boys out back."

Mildred started over, "Sonny . . . Harold . . . David . . . and hey . . . Monroe, come on . . . it's time to eat."

Sonny got up slowly from where he was sitting on the porch. He had the

20

whooping cough and he didn't look too good. Mildred said, "Mama's calling, Sonny . . . it's time to eat." Mildred walked around back just in time to see Ruby throw a big dirt clod that exploded when it hit Harold in the back of the head.

Ruby laughed.

Harold ran right at her muttering something that didn't make sense. When he got close he tried to grab her but Ruby twisted him around and got him in a head lock and bulldogged him down to the ground.

Harold yelled, "You better get off me, girl . . . I'm going to hurt you."

Ruby squeezed tighter, "Yeah . . . you and whose army?"

"Ow . . . . Ok, Ok, I quit . . . let go, I quit."

But, instead of letting Harold go, Ruby said, "Who won Harold?"

"C'mon Ruby now let me up . . . I'm not kidding."

"Say it . . . c'mon, say it . . . who won?"

"Ok . . . Ok . . . you did . . . you won . . . now, let me up."

As they both got up off the ground Harold was telling Ruby, "Don't you ever hit me with a rock again."

"It weren't no rock . . . and what are you going to do if I do?"

Ruby was a tom boy, and she was tough. Ruby was always picking a fight with Harold for the slightest thing, at all. Harold decided to take this opportunity to put a stop to it and this was not a good time because, just as Janelle turned the corner of the house and started to call out, Harold reared back and punched Ruby right-square in the stomach. It knocked the air out of her and as soon as she could catch her breath, she started crying.

"Harold Junior Anderson . . . come here, boy. Get in the house Ruby . . . . not you Harold, you come with me."

Janelle rarely whipped the kids, but for Harold to hit a girl, that was too much for Janelle to tolerate. She "blistered" Harold's bottom with a good size switch. The beating she gave him was bad enough that Harold never hit any of his sister's again. But, neither did Ruby ever try to beat Harold up again after that punch to the stomach.

After dinner, Monroe left for the square in Dahlonega. David and Sonny went outside to play and the girls helped with the dishes and with feeding Sylvia. Harold and Janelle sat at the table. It appeared as though Janelle hung back from doing any chores or from cleaning up so that she could spend that time with Harold. When Janelle gave a whipping she never held back but she always felt bad about it later.

She reached across the table and brushed the hair back out of Harold's eyes, "Hey, baby, how did you do in school today?"

"Oh Mama . . . nothing's changed . . . them rich kids don't like me much. Why is that, Mama?"

Janelle leaned forward on the table and took one of Harold's hands and for a very long moment she held his little hand pressed firmly in both of hers. She looked him straight in the eye and smiled and Harold smiled back. Harold felt safe and free from all the trouble and all the confusion that had been coming his way lately.

There were a lot of kids at home and so it was always special for Harold when his mother had time to pay attention to him. He could have sat and held his Mother's hand forever, and sometimes he thought she probably felt the same. She patted him on the back of his hand as she stood up and said, "Don't you pay it no mind, boy. They just being what they are . . . that's all."

Janelle picked up a broom and started to sweep out from under the table. As Harold lifted his feet he asked, "Mama . . . do you know that old man with the cabinet shop . . . Louis Roberts?"

"Sure do . . . why?"

Harold told his mother of all the things he heard about Louis Roberts and asked her if it was all true. Janelle laughed, "Well, I don't know, Harold. I think it's true about him being the first one in Dahlonega with electricity . . . but I can't see electricity coming to just one person in a town without others having it, too. A lot of people were here when Dahlonega got electricity and I do believe it's true that Louis Roberts was one of the first."

"What is a cabinet shop, Mama?"

"Oh Harold . . . it's . . . it's . . . just beautiful. They make all kinds of beautiful things for the home. They make it all out of wood . . . everything from cabinets to cedar chests, kitchen tables . . . and everything you can think of. They have such nice things in there. You ought to go by there and take a look someday, Harold. I'm sure Mr. Roberts would love to show you around."

Harold was listening to his Mama's words but he wasn't really hearing them. His mind was off somewhere making a decision, quite independent of his Mama's suggestion. He was already plotting a course in his mind right then as to when the earliest would be that he could go by and see Louis Roberts' place. Harold's idle curiosity grew to a sudden burning desire to learn what magic goes on inside Louis Roberts' cabinet shop.

Four

School Pictures

From the first day of school up to the very last, Harold was introduced to and reminded of the cruel differences between being rich and being poor. He never thought about it at home, it never occurred to him that he was poor. But at school all the kids wore shoes and they had nice clothes and then, there were those big kids who would bully him because he didn't.

The teacher's name was Miss Adams and it seemed to give her pleasure to urge the other kids to ridicule Harold. It was handy and more humiliating to have him sit in the front of the class so that Miss Adams could make him the target for her jokes and cruel remarks.

One day Miss Adams was handing out the school pictures that were taken two weeks before. She stood in front of Harold's desk at the front of the room and said, "Ok class, when I call your name come up front and give me your quarter and get your school picture." She called everyone's name except Harold's. She waited until after everyone else had their school picture and then she held Harold's picture up in the air, and with a smirk on her face, she looked at the other kids while addressing Harold and said, "Now, Harold Anderson, I don't suppose *you* got a quarter for your picture, do you?"

Then, she looked at Harold and waited for his answer, "No, Ma'am"

She turned back to the rest of the kids in the class and said, "Let this be a lesson" and held Harold's school picture in the air . . . "When you don't even have . . . *a quarter* . . . to pay for your school picture, this is what happens to them" and she threw his picture in the trash.

Everyone laughed.

A confused look came over Harold's face and he tried hard to figure out what he did that was so wrong and why people would laugh at him for not having a quarter. He lowered his head and felt the blood rush to his face and he just wanted to cry. But he wouldn't do it. He wouldn't allow the others in the room see him breakdown, and so he held it back, and because he did, he felt a swelling of pride in his chest replace his urge to cry. He knew then, that he was better than all those others who looked down on him.

He wanted to say, "Miss Adams, why do you want me to hate you so?"

But he kept his thoughts to himself.

No matter what happened anymore, he always kept his thoughts to himself. He always was the quiet type, more so than most. But now, he doesn't say anything because he's afraid to talk. He doesn't feel that he has anything to say that interests anyone. Most of the time, he doesn't even feel he has the right to speak up and say what's on his mind. When Miss Adams threw Harold's class photos away, he felt he had no right to say a word about it, and so he just lowered his eyes and stared at the trash can as a red flush spread over his face.

At 'recess' the class went out to play; and so, when no one was watching, Harold snuck away. He just walked off into the woods and stayed off the road in case someone might come looking for him. He didn't want to be scolded for leaving school and it would be unbearable for him if he had to stay.

After Harold was a good distance from the school he walked down to the creek, and as if absent mindedly unaware that it was freezing cold outside, he leaped over the wafer thin patches of ice and landed on a large smooth stone in the center of the creek. Harold stood still for just a moment and watched the water moving rapidly around the stone but he didn't give much thought to what it was he was watching; his thoughts were about school.

The first year in school wasn't anything like he thought it would be and nothing changed after that. The bullies still beat on him, all the kids laugh at him, and the teachers don't hide the fact that Harold is thought to be *"poor white trash"* . . . a phrase Harold has heard often in reference to himself. He doesn't fully understand what it means, but he knows that whatever it means, it is the reason he doesn't fit in.

He shrugged, "Oh well" and although he was barefooted in the freezing cold he started jumping from rock to rock down the creek. Harold discovered that by being quiet and slipping away, he was able to find himself in a world where he felt safe. He lost the enthusiasm he once had for school and so he stayed away from school as much as he could. That was one way he was able to avoid the bullies and the humiliation.

When Harold reached the dry wash leading up to Louis Robert's cabinet shop, he jumped to dry ground and headed up the hill. There was something special about Louis Roberts' place that drew Harold to it more frequently than he knew why. It might have been because Louis Roberts was the first person in Dahlonega to get electricity which gave him the power to build things out of wood and Harold was curious as to how that was done.

Harold passed by the cabinet shop a lot lately and sometimes he saw Louis Roberts coming out, or going in, but neither Harold nor Louis said much more than "Hello", or "Sure is a nice day" and "Yep, sure is" and kept moving to where ever they were going. As curious as he was to know what Louis Roberts did in that shop, Harold wouldn't stop and ask, he was too afraid. But today, as he passed the Cabinet Shop Harold had no curiosity at all in his head about anything but why people wanted to treat him the way they do.

"Hey, boy,"

The voice startled Harold, "Huh?"

"Over here."

Even with his huge shoulders stooped forward slightly, Louis Roberts filled the doorway of his cabinet shop. "You're Harold Anderson, aren't you son? I know you folks . . . you all live down on Wimpy Mill road, right?"

"Yes sir . . . Harold Anderson."

The deep lines etched in Louis Roberts' weather beaten face, when added to his size, gave Louis Roberts' a rugged appearance, but before he even spoke, his smile revealed that there was a gentle nature about this man. Harold's fear of talking to Louis Roberts was gone the minute he smiled and Harold saw Mr. Roberts as a big, gentle man, who talked softly and had the clearest eyes. When he talked to you he looked right at you; not just at the surface of you, and not through you, but right at you as though he could see who you really were.

Harold stared at what Louis Roberts was holding. He couldn't make out what it was.

Louis Roberts held it out and said, "Feel this Harold."

Harold ran his hand over it, "Wow, that's smooth . . . what is it?"

"It's walnut Harold; it's a fine piece of wood . . . walnut." As Louis spoke his eyes lit up.

Harold asked, "What's it for?"

Louis smiled, "Got a minute?"

Harold's eyes widened, "Sure."

"Then, come on . . . let me show you something."

Harold's heart was racing. This was the most Harold has ever heard Louis Roberts speak to anyone. Harold had been scared to let anyone know he wanted to see what goes on in the cabinet shop. He didn't think he had the right to ask such a thing. Harold was surprised how easy it was to be around Louis Roberts and what's more, Louis Roberts made Harold feel important just by taking the time to talk with him . . . no one has ever done that before.

Harold stepped up and went inside, "Wow!"

Louis Roberts stood back and smiled as he quietly watched Harold's expression.

The shed extended quite a bit beyond what was seen from the outside. It was filled from end to end with shiny steel and heavy black iron tools, bins of various sizes of wood, and shelves stocked with cans of paint and lacquer and varnish. There was a deep rich smell of freshly cut pine and cedar.

Harold walked past a wheel lathe and through the wood chips a foot deep on the floor and stood in front of a strange looking square "German Stove" used to dry wood before gluing and veneering. Pieces of wood the size and shape of chair legs, lamp posts, and other unfinished projects were stacked against one wall . . . this was Louis Roberts' cabinet shop.

When Harold saw this, he looked toward Louis Roberts and they both smiled and just at that exact moment, a feeling struck Harold for which no words exist. The *craftsmanship of Louis Robert's* and *Harold's appreciation for it* connected and a bond was formed between Harold and his desire to do this type of work.

He didn't know exactly what it was that made him like everything he saw as much as he did, but Louis Roberts knew exactly what Harold was feeling. Louis Roberts liked watching the enjoyment he saw in Harold and he couldn't help but recall the first day he felt the same.

Louis Roberts invited Harold into his cabinet shop and Harold stayed most of the day. As a matter of fact, it was rather late before he left, and before he did, he asked, "Pardon me Mr. Roberts, but would it be alright to come back tomorrow?"

Louis Roberts nodded, "Sure thing, son . . . you come back anytime." Harold noticed the pleasure this old man found by introducing Harold to a something new. When Harold saw that look on Louis Robert's face, Harold felt something new about himself . . . it was a feeling of being important to someone . . . and that felt good.

Five

Ugly Brogans

Henry Anderson saw a potential in Harold that he didn't see in the other boys, and he assumed it would take root and grow as a natural result of Harold staying in school. Harold took two years to get through first grade and two years for second grade and another two years to get through third grade. Harold was eleven years old in fourth grade and he was the only Anderson boy that made a sincere effort to make it good in school.

Harold helped with the farming and once in a while he helped with the still and there just wasn't time enough to put much extra effort into school. With all that he missed on the days he skipped school it was harder for him to understand what they were trying to teach on the days that he went. In time, he fell so far behind that it seemed impossible for him to ever catch up.

And then, there was a lot of time put in learning the work he had been doing at the cabinet shop. Building things and working with wood is what Harold really liked to do, and so, with all that Louis Roberts was teaching him at the cabinet shop, Harold missed even more; and fell even further behind, at school.

In addition to falling behind in his studies and being made to feel stupid for not being able to keep up with the others, he was humiliated by the older kids who made fun of him. There were two boys in particular, Cotty Walden and Pappy Sullen, who would beat on him on a regular basis. They were 15 years old and to them it was fun beating on the poor boy that came to school barefoot. They would hold him down and see who could bust his head open by hitting him on the head with their class rings.

One day Harold had to run to catch the bus and as he was walking down the aisle towards the back of the bus, Pappy Sullen tripped him at the same time the bus lurched forward. That threw Harold into a seat taken by Coty Walden. Harold pulled himself back out into the aisle and Pappy Sullen got up and grabbed him in a headlock with one arm and started punching him in the face with his other hand. There wasn't anything Harold could do, the boy was bigger and definitely had the better of him.

The driver yelled back at Harold, "Get in a seat Anderson . . . you wouldn't be causing trouble if you just took your seat."

Coty Walden leaned over and said, "Yeah . . . I'll get you later, punk."

Harold looked up at his brother, Eugene, for help.

Eugene said, "Harold. I told you before . . . you better learn how to take care of yourself."

On the bus the next day, someone else tripped Harold and everyone laughed. Coty Walden leaned over and laughed, "What's wrong? Can't you see where you're going?"

It became a very common thing to do: to laugh at Harold.

The next morning Harold stood on the side of the road waiting for the bus. He had every intention of getting on the bus but when the bus driver opened the door Harold just stood and stared through the open doorway, but he didn't get on. The kids rushed over to see why Harold wasn't getting on the bus. Harold turned around and walked away. The bus driver shrugged, "Oh, well", closed the door and the bus went on down the road. Even though the frost was on the ground Harold chose to walk to school. When Harold was passing Louis Robert's place he decided to stop in and tell Louis Roberts that he would be in later after school.

Louis Roberts said, "Son . . . you don't need that there school. All you need in life is to continue working hard, just work like I see you doing here and you're going to do just fine."

Like Harold's father, Louis Roberts saw something in Harold that few other people could see. The difference was that Louis Roberts had a way of bringing something good out of Harold. Mr. Anderson thought that what he saw in Harold would eventually grow if Harold stayed in school; and so, Harold tried to please his dad but he was failing in school and where he really excelled was in his work in the cabinet shop.

Harold was so good at the work he did at the cabinet shop, Louis Roberts looked forward to Harold coming by after school and helping him. Harold got to be so busy in the cabinet shop that many times he would stop in before school and get so busy that he would miss the whole day at school and stay all day working at the mill.

There were two different men who were very important to Harold's life, at this time. Each one of these men saw a quality in Harold nobody else could see and each one of these men had their own idea how it should be developed. Once you cut through the fat and you reach the meat of the situation, the solution was the same for each man. It was education. The only way anyone is going to be able to meet a higher standard in life is through education.

But the *process* of getting the education is just as important as the education itself. The process of becoming educated has to be one that works for you rather than against you. Harold was more than merely receptive, he was intrigued, with the education he was getting by working and learning from Louis Roberts. On the other hand, any meaningful education that could have come from Harold's going to school was destroyed by the constant humiliation in the class room from his teachers and the bullying by the other students.

Harold told Louis Roberts that he wanted to stay and finish a couple projects he was working on, but there was some reason his school teacher told him to *be sure* and be in school today. Harold didn't know why, but he thought he better be there. He said, "You're right Mr. Roberts, sir, but I got to be in school today for some reason . . . the teacher said so, just to me . . . that I had to be there. I'll be in to work on my dresser right after school."

Harold ran on to school and everyone was already seated when he got there. He ran through the door and hurriedly sat down at his desk. Harold was surprised he didn't get yelled at for being late, but instead the teacher just said in a very pleasant way, "Good . . . I'm glad you made it. We got something special for you today I'm sure you wouldn't want to miss." The syrupy way the teacher spoke to him was too pleasant and that made Harold think that, maybe it would have been better if he didn't show up today. Harold was curious as to what this big mystery was, but it wasn't like Harold to ask. The teacher would have probably said something mean, anyway. So, he just waited . . . it couldn't be anything worse than anything he has had already.

After an hour into the first period the principal came into the classroom and said, "Excuse me Miss Adams and excuse me class but . . ." she looked at Harold and wrinkled her nose and pointed right at him as she said to Miss Adams, "Clean that *Anerson* boy up over there." Harold cringed to hear her slur his name. That's what people did whenever they wanted to say the name Anderson with contempt. They dropped the letter d in the name Anderson and slurred the name to a slovenly "*Anerson*".

Then in front of the whole class she said to Harold, "It's a disgrace you coming to school the way you do." And then she turned to the teacher, "Clean the boy up and get him ready, we're going to take that there *Anerson* over to the clothing store in Dahlonega and get him some shoes."

Harold was humiliated.

Harold's jaw dropped and his mind raced in a million different directions. He wanted to be something, but this wasn't what he had in mind. He didn't know why he was such a disgrace. This wasn't who he saw himself to be. He wanted to be liked and he wanted to be respected. This was one of the most embarrassing moments in his life.

Now, more than ever, Harold felt as if the other kids were looking at him like he really *was* nothing and that he really *was* just poor white trash. No one was laughing. Even the kids who always laugh at him were confused as to how they should feel about the way Harold was being treated. Everyone sat quietly and watched. It was as if they were watching Harold being run over by a Mack truck.

The principal pulled Harold by the arm, "C'mon., *Anerson*."

They returned after lunch period and Harold had on the ugliest damned shoes anyone ever saw. These shoes were symbolic of the poor hillbilly growing up in the Appalachians, they were called Brogans. Harold never compared his feet to other kids shoes but now he has something with which a comparison can be made, and he can see the difference between these Brogans and everybody else's nice little shoes, and it just embarrassed him more.

All he could see was their nice little boots and nice Levi pants that had real creases and all that stuff and then when he looked down he saw these damn ugly Brogans. Harold could only get through the day by keeping his mind on the work he needed to do at Louis Robert's cabinet shop.

The first bell rang and school was over, and as everyone waited for the final bell to ring the kids packed their school bags and threw wadded up paper at each other. Harold's seat was at the very front of the class, and so when the second bell rang, he stood up and walked straight out the door impervious to the flying blackboard eraser that barely missed him and bounced off the wall behind him. He was down the hall and out of the building before the hallways filled with all the students going home for the day.

Six

Good at wood

Harold went down the creek and cut across to Louis Roberts and went right to work on cleaning up around his workbench as he prepared to put a coat of maple stain on his dresser. He stopped what he was doing and turned towards Louis Roberts, "Do you think I'm different?"

Louis Roberts never turned a question away or made Harold feel stupid for asking it.

He knew Harold well enough to know what he was thinking.

He said, "Son, I know what it's like to be different. Everybody knows what it's like to be different, and that right there, makes you no different than anyone else. What it is . . . people are afraid to admit they're different. People think if they're *different* no one would want to be their friend. That's wrong thinking."

Harold said, "I've always been different."

"And that's a good thing . . . which one of your friends over at that school could have learned to build what you built since you been here?"

Louis Roberts knew the Andersons and therefore he was fully aware that Harold was different from his brothers. Harold didn't want to just learn how to do something, like they do in school. He didn't want to learn something just to show what he knows and therefore receive a passing grade for knowing what he learned. Harold wanted to work at what he learned to do. This is what he *wanted* to do, and had a *desire* to do, and even had a *passion* for doing. Harold's brothers didn't *want* anything . . . all's they wanted to do was whatever it took to get by for another day.

Yes, Harold *was* different.

At school everyone was trying to make out that his being different was a bad thing and that it was something to laugh at, but Louis Roberts wanted Harold to know how *good* being different can be. He pointed out to Harold that by being able to work with his hands and build things most people couldn't, he was being different from those other people and that was a good thing. Being different, in itself, isn't bad.

Some people lose themselves in their work, but Harold found himself in his, and it was the one place that he found where he did fit in . . . the one place that *he* was the king. What a leap it was from being humiliated, laughed at, and made to feel like being nothing, and then going all the way to the other side of the coin and being able to build worthwhile projects that produced an immense feeling of pride and self worth, and now Harold, at a young age, could already build things grown men couldn't.

"Listen Harold . . . what are you doing with your dresser today?"

"I'm going to put that stain on it, sir."

"Oh . . . that's good. That's one pretty piece of work you done there, Harold, really pretty. When you get your coat of stain on . . . do me a favor would you? Go out on the dock and check this here walnut for cupping, bows, crooks, or twists and then figure out how you'd organize your cuts to remove the defects from each individual piece so you won't be wasting any stock, and then come get me; don't do no cutting . . . just come get me . . . let me see what you work out."

Harold said, "Yes sir . . . I'll figure it out alright . . . and I'll come get you."

Harold pulled a huge drop cloth off the most closely finished piece of work in the shop. It was the dresser drawers that Harold was building. Harold put the stain on his dresser and then went out and looked over the shipment of walnut that came in and tried to follow what Louis Roberts taught him about stock selection, and he made some notes in his head about the stock preparation he was being tested on.

Louis Roberts looked over Harold's stock selection and was truly impressed. He said, "Right on the money, Harold. I still don't know how you figure all that out without writing anything down . . . and then you keep it all in your head." Louis shook his head in awe of what he saw Harold able to do . . . Harold was a natural when it came to working with wood.

Harold jumped up, "Hey Mr. Roberts . . . look what time it is . . . I got to go."

"If you're coming back tomorrow . . . I could use your help . . . you know, stacking this walnut up . . . and, oh yeah, I got several sheets of back board . . . *ash* back board . . . you can do some rough cuts for me."

"I don't know sir, my dad's got sugar coming in . . . and . . . and if not, I might best be showing my face more at school . . . got to run, sir . . . can't be late."

The screen door slammed behind Harold and he ran up to the road and then walked the rest of the way back to the house.

Seven

Gun at Dinner

The routine, at the Anderson house at dinner time, was that the kids would sit at the table with their hands in their lap. Mr. Anderson didn't allow them to reach for the food, put their hands on the table, or to even speak unless they were spoken to.

Those were the rules.

Janelle said, "Your father said he'd be right in . . . we'll wait."

They all sat still listening for what they knew was to come, and then they stiffened at the scuffling sound of his footsteps coming up the stairs, and their eyes opened wide, because they all knew Mr. Anderson had been filling gallon jugs with moonshine and he had been drinking all afternoon, and they knew their father was drunk. A full minute passed after the scuffling noise on the porch stopped and it was quiet on the porch. Everyone at the table sat still and held their breath . . .

And then, there was a loud crashing sound on the door and it flew open.

Henry stood in the opening while everyone sitting at the table kept their eyes down and didn't dare to look towards the door. But, it was too much for Harold's curiosity . . . he couldn't resist lifting his head and sneaking a peek towards the door and he saw his father standing in the doorway, staring at everyone at the table.

Henry Anderson came through the door, "What are you looking at Harold?"

Janelle said, "Now dear, he didn't mean to . . ."

Henry yelled, "Shut up." And, as he took his seat he pounded both fists down onto the table causing everyone to jump at the noise. When Henry Anderson got drunk it was as though he was possessed with an evil spirit.

Everyone kept their eyes down and their hands in their lap. The smell of whiskey and sweat filled the room the minute Henry came in. Everyone sat in silence for what seemed to be a long time to not be doing something. But they waited, as was the rule, for their father's permission to start eating.

Finally Henry said, "Go on . . . eat" but when Harold looked up he saw his father come out of his pocket with a loaded gun, "You little bastards . . . I'm . . . I'm going to . . ." and he began wave the gun around the table without aiming at anyone in particular. He was just pointing the gun and saying, 'And . . . you, too . . . I'll kill every one of you . . . you, little bastards."

"Oh no, Henry . . . no," Janelle screamed, "Don't . . ." she jumped over the corner of the table and wrapped both hands around the gun. She couldn't pull it out of Henry's hand and so she put her finger through the trigger guard so Henry couldn't pull the trigger.

Henry tried to wrestle the gun loose from her grip, "Let loose damn it . . . I'm going to shoot you all . . ." and Henry pulled the trigger so hard he nearly broke Janelle's finger, but she kept her finger in the trigger guard. Harold's older brother, George, jumped in and tried to help Janelle. He grabbed Henry and tried wrestling the gun away from him. Harold saw the fire in his father's eyes and knew that he had every intention of killing everyone sitting at the table. But, Janelle's finger in the trigger guard kept Henry from pulling the trigger back while Janelle and George trying to wrestle the gun away from Henry.

Janelle was screaming, "No . . . Henry Anderson . . . no. Let loose . . . stop this right now."

With both Janelle and George wrestling Henry, their chairs tipped over sideways and they all fell to the ground.

Harold knew instantly what to do . . . he got up and ran.

He ran outside and hid in the barn and as soon as he caught his breath he realized he was the only one who had enough sense to get out and get away. Except for George the others were too scared to move. This is when Harold realized; it will always be his own decisions that he is going to follow. He knew, right then, that if he was going to survive in this world he will have to do what he thinks is right. Harold was on what he called, "a path of individuality" and he was glad that he was not like the others. He knew without a doubt that if his father would have got the gun loose he would have killed everybody there.

Harold knew what his dad would do when he was drunk. And so, by running and hiding, Harold figured that he would have been the only one to survive.

The commotion was over and not one shot was fired, thanks to Janelle. The lights were out. It was quiet and everyone else had gone to sleep. Harold, though, was still in the barn and something new had been added to his life. He didn't know how to put it, except that he felt more in control of what happens to him. That was a comfortable thought to have and so Harold closed his eyes and as quickly as he did, he fell asleep.

A large degree of innocence and blind trust fell from Harold, tonight. He realized, now, that promises are going to be lost if he waits for others to do what he must do for himself. This might be one of the lessons that taught Harold to take control of his life; and, that if he ever expects to be the king of any throne, the crown that he wears will have to be won entirely on his own.

Possibly, *that* is what he learned tonight.

When his father sobers up he won't remember a thing of what he did, but Harold will. And Harold's way of thinking, with regards to doing what would win favor with his father, has just changed. Few things in anyone's life could, in one single act, force one to grow up quicker than expected. But, a father pulling a gun at the dinner table in order to kill his whole family, maybe something like that could very well change a lot of things in a young boys mind.

Ironically though, Harold's relationship with his father was actually better after the experience with the gun at the dinner table; not because of it, or in spite of it . . . just after it. Because the realization Harold was forced to face was this . . . *when it no longer mattered to him whether, or not, he mattered to anyone else . . . Harold was free* from the distractions that kept one from perfecting his performance.

The strength of his performance became Harold's foundation for acceptance. People accepted "what he got done" easier than they accepted him, and so he became very good at whatever he set his mind to do. People accepted what he did first; and then, they accepted him.

But, whether anyone else accepted him or not, Harold found his key to success would be in his ability to accept himself. Harold was shown a dozen different times in a dozen different ways that there was only one person on whom he could rely, only one person he could trust come hell or high water, and that one person was himself.

Eight

Blowing up the Still

Henry Anderson didn't remember what he did at dinner the night before and seeing that Janelle's hand had turned a dark purple and was swollen, he shook his head. "Damn Janelle, look at your hand."

Janelle shrugged it off. "Aaah . . . ain't nothing Henry . . . it won't get in my way."

"Good. We won't be going to the market till later anyway. I'm going in town. Call Doc Grizzle. Have him look at your hand."

Harold was coming in from the barn as his dad was getting in the pick-up, "Harold, get on to school. I got business in town today."

Harold hated school but he knew better not to argue with his dad. So, Harold just stood there and watched his dad drive off and until his dad's truck was out of sight; and then, Harold slowly turned and started walking to school.

Henry Anderson was only a mile down the road when he spotted some trucks parked in a clearing near Cane Creek. When Henry pulled over to take a look he spotted a white van with government license plates parked further into the bushes. Ben Fowler's still was buried in the side of a ridge, near there, but further down by the creek. Henry didn't see Ben anywhere and so he figured something wasn't right.

He got out and walked quietly down the ridge.

He didn't go far before he saw a handful of men in the hardwoods off the creek. They were standing and marveling at Ben Fowlers handiwork. They didn't know whose handiwork it was they were admiring, but they had spent all night squatting in the leaves, sodden and cold, in a fruitless wait for the still's builder to return. The sudden hurrying of activity from the men was a sign that the waiting was over and something else was getting ready to take place.

The still was roughly the size of a tool shed and it was wedged into the dug-out ground on the side of a hill. The green galvanized roofing, mash box, and the condenser with 144 copper coils, were spray-painted green and brown in a camouflage pattern.

Henry shifted his attention to the four men milling around. A Lumpkin County deputy sheriff was taking orders from the Federal Agent that looked to be in charge. The Federal Agent was a short man with a baseball cap with big letters across the front; ATF. He wore mirrored sunglasses and kept his face towards the camouflaged section of dug out ground. He squatted down in front of a box with wires running to the still, and in a loud voice as if some justification was needed for his actions, he shouted, "When you see somebody putting this much effort into a still; like we have here, they're not doing it just for a hobby,"

Then, he shouted louder, "Fire in the hole".

All, who were standing, quickly squatted and covered their ears. Even Henry Anderson, who was further away than all the other men, grabbed his ears *and* squatted as Ben Fowler's still lit up the sky like a giant roman candle and fired a mixture of copper, sugar, and mash straight up in the air, and with it, hunks of camouflaged tin and splintered pieces of wood.

The initial sharp crack was followed by the deep muffled roar coming from within the billowing black smoke ... **Ka-Boom** ... and although a sudden jolt was felt beneath their feet, not one man moved as they watched bags of sugar being ripped apart and pieces of aluminum being hurtled skyward and tumbling through the air like flipped coins. At one final point, each man let loose the breath he was holding as the torn bags settled like old rags on the bare branches of the trees whose leaves had scattered like pigeons.

Inexplicable as it was, no one could do anything but shake their head and wonder at what they felt as they witnessed these two masterpieces of work; both were by design, and one was the other's misfortune.

Mr. Anderson got into his car and continued on towards town.

Harold Junior Anderson was on the mountain ridge a mile or so away when he thought he heard the noise of a rifle being shot and he looked across the tops of the trees in the valley below and saw the thin grey line of smoke rising a good distance away towards town. Harold shrugged, "Aw, . . . I know what that is" and he turned back and continued on to school.

Harold was passing the Mill and saw Louis Roberts, "Hi, Mr. Roberts."

"Hey Harold, are you coming to work already this morning?"

"No sir . . . I'll be in after school."

"Son, you don't need no school . . . what about that dresser you're working on . . . it's almost finished, isn't it?"

Harold said, "I know. I'll get to it, but Daddy's been on me about school lately."

Louis Roberts started waving his hand like he was shooing away a fly, "No son, you don't need to go to school today, you need to help me in the cabinet shop today. Do something that makes sense."

"I will sir . . . I will," Harold was firm, "but today it's got to be after school . . . you know how my daddy gets."

"Well tell me, Harold . . . did you hear old Ben Fowler's still going up?"

"How do you know it was Ben Fowler's?"

"I don't but I bet it was . . . the only one I know . . . built too close to the creek."

Harold was curious, "Why? What's wrong with that . . . the still needs water . . . how could being too close to the creek be bad?"

"Well Harold it's too easy to find your still that way. The Feds . . . they got branch waders; that's all they do is wade through all the creeks searching for the pipes that's running water to the liquor stills. All they have to do is follow the pipe right to your still. But, you know what we did back in the day? We would run pipe out for miles to nowhere just to make the branch waders wonder if a pipe was for real before following it. Sometimes they would come across a pipe that was for real but they wouldn't follow it, thinking it was going to take them on a chase. Some of the folks up in the mountains would take their water pump off their well and use it to pump water up from the creek. But you got to be careful Harold . . . it's the water that will lead the feds right to you."

"How about you Mr. Roberts sir . . . you have a still anywhere's?"

"Oh, back in the day, Harold . . . back in the day. It's a thing of the past, you know. It's dying out. The government's going to crack down on bootlegging and moonshine some day . . . you just watch." "Louis Roberts had a sound that bordered on regret about the changes taking place in the world.

He shook his head as he thought of all this progress the 60's was bringing to Dahlonega. Louis Roberts watched Harold run down the hill and jump the creek in the direction of school and wondered if this change was ever going to do anyone any good.

Nine

Quit school

In those earlier years of going to school barefoot and in raggedy clothes no one wanted to be mistaken for Harold's friend and so everyone stayed away from him. But, when Harold was a teenager he had his own circle of friends. The bullies were still around but they had to be more careful with how they went about bullying Harold because he didn't mind taking a whipping and, more often than not, he chose to get whipped before he was going to get pushed around.

The crowd Harold ran with got into their fair share of mischief but the major difference between Harold's hoodlum buddies and the other gangs in Dahlonega was that Harold and his friends never let mischief get in the way of their work. If they had a job to do, whether it was fixing a fence, working the farm, stealing a car, or running whiskey, they did their work first and then, they went off to raise hell.

Harold was proud of the fact that he could earn money now, and he liked buying the clothes that he wanted to wear. He also bought his own car, and he always had money in his pocket. With what he learned at the mill from Louis Roberts, Harold was able to make money doing odd jobs and fixing things. He acquired a work ethic from his father and the skill to build and fix things from Louis Roberts. This was a winning combination that paid off for Harold.

The boys Harold hung around with were much like him when it came to working. They worked, every one of them, and none of them was a drain on anyone. They didn't go for unemployment, or welfare, or a hand-out of any kind. They sure as hell weren't angels, they screwed up a lot but they got their work done first, and if they had time after that, then; they screwed up.

Harold was still in school during the time he started working and earning money. Harold agreed with how Louis Roberts felt about his going to school but his dad wanted him to finish school and so he stayed and tried to make it through. In the time that Harold worked at the mill Although Louis Roberts was very open about his opinion. He never tried to pressure Harold to quit school but he never failed to take the opportunity to say what he thought about school being a waste of time for Harold, either.

In the few years that Harold was doing work around the mill, Louis Roberts appeared to have aged quickly. He was still big and strong but he was a little more stooped over and he walked a little slower than he used to walk. But Louis Robert's age showed the most when he would impart some philosophical statement to Harold as if throwing one last Hail Mary for Harold to catch in the end zone . . . one last jewel of wisdom that Louis Roberts hoped would help Harold's life go in the direction Louis Roberts felt it should go. Harold heard it a dozen times if he heard it once, "Son, being educated and having a lot of book learning will get you no where. It's more important to be an honest person and work hard and you'll get everything you need out of life."

As hard as Harold tried to stay in school for his father Harold continued to fall behind in the things he was supposed to learn, because he was still missing a lot of school. He didn't miss so much school as a result of the bullying anymore or because of the ridicule. The humiliation was still hanging on like a stigma, but most of the time, he missed school because he was just too damn tired from working. He did the chores around the farm when he got home from school and sometimes he helped Louis Roberts and then many times he was working all night on the still. At fifteen years old Harold was usually out somewhere, doing something to make money, and the next day he would be in school. And then, after school he would go right through the same routine; doing the chores on the farm, building something or fixing something for somebody, and then going out that night and doing whatever could be done to make more money.

One day, after working all night, Harold was in school and he was tired. He just wanted to close his eyes for a minute, and so laid his head down on his desk, and it felt so good. With every breath he exhaled he felt the weight of his head and his shoulders sink deeper into his forearms that were sprawled on the top of his desk.

The teacher asked the class a question and one of the students answered. In reference to that student's response the teacher asked, "And, Harold, what do you think? Is that right . . . was it Thomas Jefferson? Harold . . . hellooo Harold . . ."

The teacher placed her finger to her lips to signal the class to be quiet. She grabbed the yard stick from the black board's trough and tip toed to the back of the room. Then, she came up behind Harold quietly . . . the other kids were so excited they started to be noisy, almost spoiling the teachers plans. Harold stirred and shifted a little bit in his seat and then settled his head back into the comfort of his folded arms. A few of the girls were holding their hands across their mouths to keep from laughing out loud.

Standing directly over Harold, the teacher reared back with the hand that was holding the yard stick and then came forward with it, as hard as she could, and smacked Harold on the back of the head with the yard stick so hard that it broke in two. The sound, alone, was loud enough to wake anyone . . . . *Zaa Rap.*

A thin stream of electricity shot through Harold's nervous system and he shot up out of his seat and stood stiff as a board and was suddenly more bright eyed and alert than he had been for days. Harold was embarrassed more than hurt, but the shock of waking up like that sent a cold chill through his chest causing him to gasp sharply, inhale deeply and hold his breath.

And then, the teacher yelled at him, "Harold Anderson, you will *never* amount to anything in your life. You are nothing now, and you will always be nothing. You don't finish assignments, you don't even know what homework to do because you're never here . . . and when you are here, look at you Harold, how do you think it makes me feel that you fall asleep in my class. Am I that boring to you? Harold, you're just a bum and a hoodlum."

This was a rude awakening . . . but it was a welcome awakening just the same!

That rap on the back of my head made me so clear headed that I knew exactly what I was to do before she said her last word. I was already standing in the middle of this class room and as I looked around at these little "goody two shoe" kids, all smug and righteous, I thought; "Hell they ain't even got a clue".

They have no idea what's going on around them or what it's going to take to make it in this world. What's worse, is this poor excuse for a teacher whose job it is to teach this to them, and she doesn't even know from a bucket of rocks herself.

I thought about the $300 in my pocket and I wanted to ask the teacher how much she had in her pocket right now and when was the last time she had money to blow on whatever she wanted. I know it's different today than it was when she was 15 years old, this is the 60's and $300 doesn't buy what it did in the fifties; but still, none of these idiots who laugh at me has ever had this kind of money in their pocket, and I can make this kind of money every day, if I wasn't here.

For the first time in my life I am awake. As I stood there in the middle of the class room everyone, including the teacher, was dead still. No one said a word and no one moved. Every eye was fixed on me. They were waiting to see why I was standing, or if I was going to say anything. I was thinking that now is my time, this is my chance to say anything I want and not get in trouble for it. I could tell these kids off, these kids who laugh at me, who the hell do they think they are? I could even tell this teacher what a fucking joke she is, and what a terrible person she turned out to be. But I chose not to say anything. They wouldn't understand it anyway and I would only be wasting my breath.

So, I put it very simple, and I said, "I'm walking out of here . . . I quit."

I quit school but I didn't quit education, because from that day forth I considered myself an entrepreneur. I taught myself to read what I needed to read and I taught myself to write what I needed to write. When it comes to algebra or calculus though, I'm dumber than a bucket of rocks. But, I can compute how much lumber it takes to build a 45,000 sq ft club and not waste a stick, and everything I touch turns to gold and I'm good at counting gold.

My dad will just have to understand . . . being in school didn't mean I was being educated; I was being humiliated for being poor, I was being bullied for not giving in to the crowd, and I was being laughed at for trying to overcome the setbacks in my life.

When I walked out of that school room it was like a big load was lifted from my shoulders. I felt like I was a free man. I couldn't wait to get down the hill and across the creek and see *the Old Man at the Mill*, my friend Mr. Louis Roberts.

Hell, it felt good to tell Louis Roberts, "I quit school".

But the look I got from him when I told him wasn't what I expected it to be. I thought he would be real happy but he just nodded as if he already knew. I thought he'd be happily surprised and say things that would show that he was pleased with me. But he just nodded and said, "Good. Are you going to finish that night stand, today?"

I said, "Oh yeah" and went inside to work.

Thirty minutes later Louis Roberts called to me from outside. When I went outside Louis Roberts was sitting on a stump. I never saw him so spent. He didn't look tired. He just looked *used up* in a peaceful sort of way. Louis Roberts stood up and said, "Harold, let's walk to the creek."

There was no purpose for it . . . there was nothing to carry to the creek and nothing to carry back, we weren't going there to cut down a tree, or to blow up a beaver's dam. This was a different Louis Roberts than the one I knew. I never saw him go anywhere or do anything for which there wasn't a specific purpose. But today, Louis Roberts said he just wanted to walk down the hill to the creek and so I followed.

Neither of us talked along the way but when we reached the creek Louis Roberts sat down on the bank and said, "Sit down boy. There's something I want to tell you."

I sat down and settled back against the trunk of a tree.

Louis Roberts said, "Son, I know this was a big decision for you to make today, quitting school. You know what *my* views are . . . about school and all. I know I told you my views a lot but I said them as simply as I could so as not to push you in one direction or the other. But just in case I did, let me give you another thought. Your brothers quit school and I think that was a dumb thing for them to do . . . you quit school and I think that was a smart thing for you to do."

I sat there and thought about it . . . but I didn't really catch on to what he meant.

Louis asked me, "Do you see what I'm saying?"

"Uh uh . . . no I don't."

"You're brothers . . . they had no drive, no ambition. They didn't want anything . . . staying in school *might* have helped them . . . they had nothing to lose by staying in school . . . they were already losers and so being out of school they're still lost. School might have done something for them, and" Louis Roberts shrugged, "maybe not."

He continued, "You, on the other hand, have ambition, you got desires, you're motivated. You need to be out in the world . . . out here . . . going after what you want. The way they treating you in school . . . hell, they were beating you to death."

"I have a car now . . . maybe I should go to a different school . . . maybe in Gainesville."

"Look, I know you don't want to go against your daddy's plans . . . but I got to tell you this, it doesn't matter how much schooling you got or how smart you are or how much education you get. It ain't worth a shit unless you . . . look here Harold . . . it's who you hang around with and who you associate with that depends how far you get in life. You can be the smartest person on the planet and hang around the dumbest people and you'll never go anywhere. You can be the dumbest person on the planet and the smarter the people you a hang around with . . . the farther you will go in life."

I laughed, "The people in my bunch are a lot of fun but they're not too smart."

"Then get out of your bunch. Surround yourself with smart people and then shut your mouth, because smart people just can't wait to tell you how smart they are. Smart people will tell you how they create things and how they make money, and everything else about how they do what they do. Just surround yourself with smart people; and then shut up."

"Yeah . . . that's the truth. I've seen them do that, alright."

"Another thing son, you're good with your hands. What I see special about you is that you have a talent to do anything you put your mind to. I hope I have the time to teach you more but in case I don't . . . I would hope that of anything you might have learnt from me . . . I hope that it would be about *survival*."

"Survival?"

Louis Roberts continued, "Survival is hard work, son . . . you see, it isn't what you *talk* about doing . . . it's what you actually do that will tell the world what kind of man you are."

"What does this have to do with *survival*?"

Louis Robert's face suddenly looked cheerful, "Well son, think of survival this way. Every morning when that sun comes up, a rabbit wakes up and knows it must run faster than the fastest fox or it will be killed. And every morning when the sun comes up, a fox wakes up and knows it must run faster than the slowest rabbit or it will starve."

I got up when Louis Roberts stood and I was confused, but I waited. I knew the way he spoke. Louis Roberts always left a space for me to consider where a statement he just made, was leading. Louis Roberts put his arm around my shoulder and turned me around back towards the mill and we started walking and then he continued, "You see Harold, it doesn't matter whether you're a fox or a rabbit . . . when the sun comes up in the morning, you better be running."

Ten

Cattle Rustling

My Dad didn't like that I quit school, but he didn't have any trouble finding plenty of work for me to do around the farm, either. A major portion of any work on a farm that had a lot of livestock was building and mending fences, the barbed wire kind. I got pretty good at it and by the time I was sixteen I was known for the good work I did building barb wire fences.

One day my dad yelled for me to come in the house. The farm we lived on belonged to Mr. Harold West and he was standing with my dad on the porch when I crossed the yard. They shook hands and Mr. West left.

My dad turned to go in the house and said, "C'mon, I got something for you" and he started right in explaining what he and Mr. West had been discussing. "Mr. West needs about four or five miles of barb wire fence built and I told him you'd do it."

"Ok, when do I start?"

"Now hold on Harold, this no small job. It's going to take up most of your day, every day, and probably take up your whole summer."

"Ok, I guess I better get started then"

"Don't you want to know the best part? Mr. West is going to pay you five dollars a week, all summer long or until the job is done."

In that day, five dollars was five dollars, and that was a lot of money to me, but that wasn't what felt good. It made me feel good that here I was, 16 years old, and Mr. West chose *me* to build this fence. I guess he could have chosen my Dad or one of my older brothers, but, he chose me. The fact that I was chosen to do the job was more important to me than the money.

I wouldn't get paid until the job was done, but that was alright. I was going to need to be focused on the job anyway. I wouldn't have had time to spend the money if I had it, and I thought that would be a good way to save it up. I actually enjoyed doing the work so much that it was no time at all that the end of summer came, and the job was finished.

It wasn't easy work, we had a hot summer and I dug miles and miles of post holes. My hands were so dry and callused that when I closed them the calluses would crack open and bleed. But it was worth every bit I put into it, because I did a good job. Everyone who saw the work I did praised it, especially Mr. West, and that really made my summer.

But then, one day my daddy came in and flipped me a silver dollar, the old time type silver dollar . . . wasn't even shiny. He said, "Here son, this is from Mr. West and he told me to tell you thanks for such a fine job."

I didn't know what to say. I didn't argue with my Dad about it, as a matter of fact, I got so mad I couldn't even speak. When he left, I literally broke down and cried. It wasn't about not getting the money. It was the slap in the face statement that said my work wasn't good enough to move Mr. West to be honorable and pay me what he promised.

The slap in the face was the emotional point but there's also a practical side. Although, I didn't start the job for the money I still needed the money. I needed to get paid and if Mr. West wasn't going to pay me I was going to have to do something to get some money. I figured to go steal some cars or I could spend a week in the woods making whiskey, but then I'd have to strip the cars and sell the parts or go off and sell the liquor.

I needed money right now and both of these options would take too much time, and that's when I remembered someone told me last year, of how I could make some money real fast. At the time I thought it was dumb, but, now that I think about it, I like the idea. At least it's fast.

He told me of someone in White County who would give $75 a head for cattle; no questions asked. I got to thinking about the several hundred head of cattle we took care of for Harold West. And I thought hell, I'll just steal me some of Harold West's cattle and I'll take them to White County and sell them.

I went out in the barn and I grabbed a little bull or a little heifer, and any of them heifers or bulls that I could pick up and carry, I tied up and stuck in the back of my car and took them to White County and sold them. What got me caught was, my dad had a prize little English black and white faced bull that he wanted to raise for studding. But one day I said, "Fuck it and fuck him, too" and so I stole my daddy's prize bull and I went and sold that bitch for $75.

The next day my uncle Ralph Ridley, who was the sheriff for Lumpkin County, came by looking into why we were missing so many cattle. Well, Ralph Ridley and my dad looked around the farm and when they got around to looking into my little Camaro, I was a caught bitch. I might as well have been caught red-handed with the bull in the back seat of my car because they found cow shit, and hair, and everything else that showed I was guilty.

My dad shouted, "I knew it. That little bastard stole my bull."

They took me to jail and locked my ass up and while I was waiting for trial my dad and my brother Monroe went to White County and got my dad's bull back. Because of its unique markings they were able to identify it from the others. But it was the only one they could actually recognize as belonging to Mr. West. They couldn't tell which of the other little heifers were stolen but that didn't stop my dad from pressing charges against me for stealing his little white face bull.

I went in front of a judge out of Gainesville, Georgia named Judge Kenyon. He was a huge, tall man with grey hair, and an awfully mean look. He looked like a ghost. And there I was, 16 years old and standing in front of this ghostly looking man, in his courtroom.

Judge Kenyon looked at me strange and I wasn't sure what he was looking at. He just looked like a great big ghost looking me over. Maybe he thought I was going to run. I didn't know what he was doing. He looked at me for the longest time and then he finally said, "Son, what's wrong with your hands?"

I looked down and noticed that I was dripping blood from both of my hands on the court room floor. I said, "Well, Judge they're bleeding . . . I can't open them, because they, well they just hurt."

The blood was dripping out of the cracks of my calluses but I had white cloths wrapped around my hands. But, I was fidgeting around more nervous than normal and I kept opening and closing my hands and didn't even notice that the cracks in the calluses started bleeding again.

Judge Kenyon said, "Boy, take those rags off and let me see your hands."

I took the bandages off my hands and there were rows of calluses.

The Judge asked, "What have you been doing?"

"Your honor . . . I've been digging post holes . . . I been building a barb wire fence, sir."

"Is that your job, son?"

"No your honor . . . not really, I was doing this for my Dad and Mr. West . . . they the ones over there . . . that had me arrested."

He said, "Well Son, why are your hands like that?"

I said, "Judge . . . I dug every fence hole for a five mile stretch with a big heavy set of post hole diggers and no gloves. I done this all summer long. The calluses are from all that work and now . . . they busted open . . . they bleeding . . . and that's sort of why I'm here, now."

The Judge said, "Go ahead, son, tell me why you're here, now. I want to hear this."

"Your honor, I worked all summer for Mr. West and my dad, and they said they were going to pay me 5 dollars a week and at the end of the summer I was going to get paid for the whole summer of building his five miles of barbwire fence for all of those cattle of his."

"Did you build the fence like you said you would?"

"Yes sir."

"Did you get paid?"

"Yes sir, they paid me. But it wasn't what they were supposed to pay me."

"Well, what did they pay you, son?"

"My pay for the whole summer, your honor . . . was one dollar. I needed the money they promised to pay me to buy clothes and stuff that I needed. I earned that money."

The Judge looked over at Harold West and just stared at him and then he looked at my Dad and you could see the judge was steaming . . . you could see it in his eyes. He stared at them like, "What in the world are you doing to this kid?"

I was still standing there in front of a full courthouse with blood dripping out from both of my hands. Everyone hung on every word I said and when I quit talking you could hear a pin drop. I looked around at my Dad, at Harold West, and then I saw the look on the people's faces in the courtroom. I really thought the people in the court house was going to string my dad and Harold West up, because back then, well lynching wasn't that far gone.

The judge cleared his throat, leaned forward, and looking me straight in my eye he said, "I'm going to ask you something, son."

"Yes sir."

"Did you sell them heifers and bulls by the hoof or on the slab?"

There was a long silence in the court room as I tried to understand what he meant. I didn't know what he was talking about. Finally, I looked back up to the judge and said, "Your honor, I really don't know what you mean by *the hoofs or on the slab*."

Judge Kenyon looked at me with just a little half ass grin and said, "Well, let me rephrase my question . . . were they alive when you sold these bulls and heifers or did . . ."

"Oh, hell yeah . . . walking around like anything . . . you know, alive . . . I didn't kill nothing."

The Judge got a serious look on his face and said, "Oh well, that's not so bad then . . . that changes the whole thing." Then he leaned forward as he looked at me and said, "Son I want to ask you one more question."

I bobbed my head up and down and said, "Yes sir your honor."

"How many heifers and how many bulls, exactly, did you steal?"

Now here was a tough question. The judge has really been fair with me so far; and so, I hate to lie to him but I certainly don't want to bury myself either. So I looked up at the judge with a little grin and said, "Well Judge . . . how many did I get caught with?"

He said, "One."

I said, "Ok, that's how many I stole your honor."

The judge smiled and said, "Harold Junior Anderson, I'm giving you a fifty dollar fine and one year probation." Then he looked at Mr. West and my Dad and said, "Don't you ever let me find out that you mistreat a kid . . . don't ever mistreat a kid who comes to me . . . and as long as you live, don't you ever mistreat this boy again, either."

Eleven

My Rowdy Friends

When I quit school I didn't have to put up with the snobs and the do-gooders, and I didn't have those half-wit teachers looking down on me. I was able to work and buy the things I needed and buy the things I wanted. Because I was good at the work that I did I always had money in my pocket.

My friends were just a group of fun loving maniacs. They weren't bullies, or killers, or career criminals. They were just a rowdy crazy as hell bunch of guys. They all worked real jobs for a living even though they enjoyed stealing cars, making moonshine, and running liquor.

We had a couple places we hung out. There was an all-night speakeasy outside of town, and in town, we hung out around the square, and out past the graveyard, we hung out at an all-night gas station on Hwy 9 that goes into Dawsonville.

The man who ran the all-night gas station was a big old country man. He tolerated us hanging out there because we all bought gas and stuff from him but he didn't like us at all. He was always afraid that we'd come down and blow his station up and make a parking lot out of it . . .

That tension was bad enough to start with but to make things worse, sometimes the older bunch, Snooks Brackett, Archie Berry, and Doug Walker came around and tried to stir things up. Sometimes they succeeded, and when they did, somebody usually got hurt. And so, with all that tension around us we stayed wound up tight most of the time. We don't even know why we did half of what we did or how we lived through all the things we did . . . we just did it.

Take JC, for instance, a one of a kind character, and still to this day, I don't know his real name. But, he was crazy. He was a little fellow weighing in no more than 115 to 125 lbs. and no matter what; hot weather or cold, he wore a long trench coat that reached to the ground and underneath his coat he always carried two sawed off shotguns on a sling, one on each shoulder. He wasn't always around but where ever he showed up something crazy was going to happen.

Sometimes when he couldn't stop in at the all-night station he would go flying by at 60 or 70 miles an hour in his little Sunbeam car, and as a way of saying "Hi" to all of us, he would pull the emergency brake up and start spinning until he had done 3 or 4 donuts and then when he straightened out he'd just wave and keep on going.

One night we were all sitting on our cars and Romeo and I were showing the others how to do the Cobra wave. Romeo said, "Look here . . . grab the steering at the bottom, lean to the left and drop your left shoulder as low as you can. Bend your right elbow and while keeping your hand straight bend your wrist and you got the Cobra."

We all tried it out and Danny Brewster laughed, "I got it . . . I got it . . . how's this?"

"Yeah, that's it," I said, "Lean more . . . ok, a little more . . . that's it . . . you got it."

Romeo and I figured we just invented "the Cobra Wave."

We called him Romeo because with his personality and attitude he would always wind up with the women. He was a good looking guy weighed about 220 lbs. and just a one of a kind, good guy. He had polio when he was a kid and walked with a limp, but he was just as wild and crazy as you could get.

A lot of us had these 302 Ford Cobra cars . . . boss 28's . . . and 302 bosses, and so after we invented "the Cobra wave", anytime Romeo and I saw each other coming down the road, we would switch sides and pass each other driving on the wrong side of the road, and as we passed each other, we did the Cobra Wave.

A buddy I knew from the pool hall drove into the station and said, "Hey guys, whatzup?"

"Hey Bobby, where you been, man. We were looking for you earlier . . . we might make a run to College Park . . . you up for it?"

"I could be, but I need a new engine . . . I got my eye on a little Mustang parked down at Burlington. Help me snatch that 302 and put it in here and I'll be able to run your whiskey any where you want."

I asked, "When?"

"It's got to be right a way . . . I heard they're putting a fence up around the parking lot out at Burlington and they might even post a guard at the gate."

I said, "We need a couple more guys if we're going to drop that engine before day light."

Just then, we heard the shrill of a gear box winding its way to a high pitch. We looked and saw a little Sunbeam coming our way. JC had the gas pedal to the floor and he kept it there as the little Sunbeam was gradually but steadily picking up speed along the stretch of highway that ran past the station.

JC was on a roll tonight.

Even as it passed us it was still continuing to gain speed.

He was pushing that little Sunbeam up past 80 miles an hour and he kept the pedal to the floor until he was a good distance past the station. He was out of sight but we heard it when he yanked that emergency brake because there was the spinning and skidding and all the noise that was usually there when JC pulled that brake.

An hour later, though, JC came limping and almost stumbling into the station. He was all mangled, tattered, and torn. The side of his head was all bloody, his nose was bleeding, and both his pant legs was torn and you can see a huge open cut on his left leg. His coat was all but rip to shreds and you could see the shotguns just dangling from their slings underneath what was left of his coat.

JC was a comical character to start with but this was something else. We couldn't stop laughing as he told us in detail how he yanked up the emergency brake and started to spin, and then rolled, and then flipped that little Sunbeam of his. He described every thought he had at each step; when he spun, when he rolled, and when he flipped. And he said he flipped six times. We shouldn't have been laughing. We should have been rushing him to the hospital. But, he was laughing so hard . . . he was laughing harder than any of us, and he was getting as big kick out of telling us every little detail about flipping that little sunbeam . . . and what's more amazing about it . . . his Sunbeam was a convertible.

JC was just flat crazy . . . and, he just enjoyed doing crazy things.

Just as crazy though, was Michael Thompson. We called him Big Newton because he loved to eat them little bitty Fig Newton cookies. He was a big old baby Huey looking kind of guy . . . just crazy. But he was a lot of fun to be around. We learned not to drink beer and eat pork skins with him in a closed room, though, because he would just gas you to death. We called my little brother David, *little* Newton because David and Michael Thompson hung together a lot and they were both stoned stupid. They were always doing some dumb shit and get caught doing it.

Danny Brewster was 6 foot tall with broad shouldered and he wore his hair in a flat top and he was just a good guy. In 1971 we saw the movie Billy Jack and that's what got us interested in karate. He went on to be a world class karate kick boxer. He was my buddy and for most of our lives we got along and done a lot of wild things together.

Daniel Crow was long and lanky. He was just a funny comical person to be around and later he became a brother in law when he married my sister Shirley and then he went off to NC. He never went anywhere without his Georgia credit card, which was a five gallon gas can and a rubber hose.

Then there was High Pockets. We said he wore his pants so high that he got underarm stains on his belt loops. He was a good looking guy but he was just a comical looking character, the way he wore his pants so high. He was crazy just like the rest of us . . . and maybe a little bit more.

These were some of the friends I ran with in those days. There were other guys that would show up now and then, but whose names I don't remember. But all these guys here, they stuck with me through some pretty odd times.

I was getting ready to leave the all-night station and go over to the speakeasy, so I told Bobby that I'd help him get that car from the mill if he got a couple guys to help us drop the engine.

He said he would and told me to meet him the next afternoon at the square and we'd go over to Burlington before the day shift let out.

Michael Thompson and I left the all night station and were on our way to the speakeasy when Archie Berry ran up on us and we pulled over. Archie Berry was one of the three main bullies of Dahlonega. He ran around with my cousin Doug Walker and Snooks Brackett. He was 6'5" and weighed 250. I was much smaller than he was but my buddy Michael Thompson, who we called Big Newton, wasn't small, at all; he was a big old 240 pound baby Huey. He was a good natured guy who just didn't give a shit about anything. He was comical as hell and about half crazy but he couldn't fight a lick, and Archie Berry knew that, and that's why Archie was always pushing Newton to fight.

We were just teenagers, and Archie Berry was ten or fifteen years older than us. But, for some reason or another, trouble been brewing between Newton and Archie for a long time, and so when he drove up, Archie just happened to pull up on my side and so he looked at me when he said, "I'm just going to kick you all's ass . . . you little punks."

I looked over at Newton and we laughed, and I said, "Did you hear this mother fucker? He said he was going to kick our ass."

Newton just laughed half crazy like.

I said, "What do you think?"

Newton said, "That son of a bitch ain't going to whip nobody" and so Newton looked at me and then looked over at Archie's car and said, "You ain't going to whip nobody mother fucker and you damn sure ain't going to whip us with your lips, so get your ass out."

Archie Berry just got crazy mad; because, we were just two young guys and we were mouthing off to this big bully who thought he was a real man's man.

Now my buddy Newton always carried a little 32 pistol and I told him, over and over, "You couldn't kill a rat with a 32 pistol." But when I looked over at Newton I saw he had it in his hand and I said, "Hey . . . what are going to do with that?"

He said, "I'm going to shoot this mother fucker."

Archie Berry got out and stood up looking over the top of his car. I stayed seated and looked up at Archie and then I looked back over at Newton who was already out of the car and was throwing his arm straight across the top of my car with that little 32 caliber gun in his hand. And as soon as Newton's arm stretched across the top of my

car he shot Archie Berry dead between the eyes and dropped him . . .
BAM . . . and Archie Berry hit the ground.

Big Newton got back in the car and said, "Ok motherfucker,
nwwow what do you say about my little .32?"

I shrugged and said, "Well, hell" and we drove off and left the
bitch lay where he fell.

The next afternoon I met
Bobby down at the square.
He had two guys with him
I didn't know, but Bobby
said they were *'alright'* and
so we all went down to
Burlington and hotwired
that little Mustang and was
out of the lot in less than
thirty seconds. We drove it

to a little deserted shack in the woods, where we hid out from time to
time, and we went to work.

We lost all track of time trying to get that engine out. It was past
midnight when we finally finished, and I'll be damned, someone came
out from the brush and turned a light on us, "Harold, what you boys
got?"

I knew his voice immediately. "What the hell you doing out here,
Butch?"

"Don't act surprised, Harold. Well, look here . . . looks like I caught
you all, red handed."

Butch was a deputy sheriff but he was also my brother-in-law and
it did surprise me that he would show up here. He doesn't normally
bother us about stuff like this.

He said, "That isn't that Ford Mustang that was missing from the
parking lot out at Burlington yesterday afternoon, is it?"

"Look Butch, you have no stake in this."

"Oh . . . you boys are behind the times. Didn't you know? Things
are going to be different with Sheriff Seabolt in office? We're cracking
down on all the car thieving and the bootlegging" he paused, and then
said, "Oh yeah, and the shooting, too." Butch stopped, furrowed his
brow, and cocked his head to one side as he mimicked trying to recall
something important and then asked, "Oh yeah, did you hear about
Archie Berry?"

I stiffened up, "What about Archie Berry?"

"Someone shot him dead between the eyes."

I gave a quick nod, "Ha . . . good riddance to that piece of shit."

"Oh no . . . it didn't kill him. Someone shot him with a .32 caliber . . . the bullet split and went around the skull underneath the skin."

"Really fucked him up, though . . . huh?"

"Not at . . . it knocked him out, but when he got up, he drove himself to the hospital. They said they might put a little steel plate in his head, but from what I hear, it's not going to do any worse than leave a scar on his forehead."

I rolled my eyes and shook my head, I couldn't believe it.

Butch said, "And so, as I was saying," he paused, "What are you all doing?

"We're running."

Butch said, "Well, I'm going to make it real easy for you. I'm going to let you keep on running" then he said, "just put that engine in the trunk of my car . . . because, you see, I want that engine . . . I'll let you little bastards go on and keep on running and I won't lock your asses up."

My buddies and I looked at each other and I knew how stone crazy this son of bitch Butch was, and so we all gave the nod and said, "Ok! No problem."

We put the engine of this 302 Mustang in the trunk of his patrol car and he was going down the highway and got stopped by the State Troopers and he couldn't, for the life of him, explain why he had an engine to a stolen car in the trunk of his patrol car. The troopers didn't lock his ass up right away because he was driving the Sheriff's patrol car but after a couple weeks of investigation they brought charges against him for the Mustang that was stolen from Burlington Mills and he ended up getting five years in prison. Butch tried to name us as the thieves, but there was no proof against us, and although we got away with it, the Sheriff knew the real story.

Twelve

Butter Milk Biscuit

We were not a gang.

When we were in our teens we were just a bunch of hoodlums.

We acted independently from each other and sometimes we worked some jobs together; but, for the most part, we were all a little crazy in our own way. We were just a wild bunch of boys who ran together. One thing I can honestly say about my buddies was that we all worked. None of my friends were lazy or laid around asking for a handout. We made our own money from the jobs we worked, nobody gave us anything. Each one of the boys I ran with was a success in their own right.

We may have been crazy little bastards but we didn't mean anyone any harm. We never bothered anyone who didn't deserve it. But now, if they deserved it, that was different. And the North Georgia ranger camp . . . they deserved it. We were tired of them coming into town and stealing our pussy. All those soldiers would be coming down to our town and nailing our little bitches, and we didn't like that, so we would just shoot at them. We didn't try to hit them, we just shot to scare them off, running back to their camp. We did that every time they came to town until the camp made Dahlonega off limits to the Rangers and they left our little bitches alone.

We were a rough crew, but I'll repeat myself . . . we were *not* a gang.

We never were like these punk ass gangs you got in the city, today, that are getting all drugged up and selling drugs to little kids. Those punks don't have a work ethic or even know what work is. They're nothing but a low life bunch of gangsters. They call themselves a gang but then they steal from each other, rat on each other, and roll over and stab each other in the back. They thrive on hurting and stealing from, cheating and lying to, people who are smaller and weaker than they are . . . punk ass gangs today are nothing but sorry ass bullies.

From time to time, we . . . the boys I run with . . . we butt heads with each other, too. But we have honor and respect. We're not going to steal from our own, we don't shit where we sleep, and if we tell you we have your back, we do. And if we say we're going to blow your head off, we will. We stand up and face you man to man and let you know what's going down, and you can count on what we say.

And, like I say, we worked hard . . . at every thing we did . . .

Some of us had farm work to do with the corn, potatoes, lettuce and all the other produce. We had chickens, hogs, horses, and we had the cows to milk. Some of us had day jobs working in or around town, but whatever it was; we worked hard at it and we were good at what we did. Then, when the work was done we went out at night running moonshine, stealing cars, doing whatever we do, and raising hell with the girls.

My favorite thing was hauling whiskey. I didn't drink whiskey. I saw what whiskey did to my Dad and I swore I wasn't going down that road. But, boy did I have fun hauling that stuff. The money was alright but that wasn't why I ran moonshine. I liked running those fast cars on the back roads of the north Georgia hills and outrunning the law. It was just the wild excitement of it all.

But, it was just as much fun to come right through town with it, too.

I'd get a whole load of pretty girls and stuff them in my 62 Pontiac Catalina convertible and my trunk would be full of whiskey. My convertible was baby blue with a white top and the girls loved riding with me through town when I was carrying a load of whiskey. The top would be down and I would have so many pretty little girls in my car you couldn't fit another one in. I had a couple girls sit up on the back of the front seat and have their legs draped around my neck.

My girls would be flirting with the deputies and it make them just go crazy trying to get some pussy. The deputies didn't even think about the load of whiskey I was carrying. Some of the deputies didn't think I'd be hauling whiskey with that load of bitches in my car. The ones who knew I was hauling whiskey didn't care, they was looking to get some pussy and didn't give a damn about catching me with the liquor. They knew what I was doing. My cousin was a deputy and he knew my game, They all knew what we were doing, but the police and the deputies were either family, or they were in on the liquor run with us, or else we just flat paid them off.

One day, after my whiskey run, I was driving through the square. I had dropped off all my whiskey and sent all the pretty girls home and I was by myself. I pulled over in front of the pool hall when I saw Joey King coming around the square.

Damn she was a raving beauty. But, whenever she was around, I paid her no attention. She comes from a rich family and she was the most popular girl in school. I sure would like to be with someone like her, but I had no chance at that happening, and so I never paid any attention to her. Today, when she pulled up along side of me I casually looked her way, and when I did, she flipped me the bird and then stomped on the gas and tore off.

I thought, "Shit, I'll whip this bitches ass" and I took off after her. She was just running wide open, laughing and having a good ol' time, but I ran her down and caught up with her at the swimming pool. When I walked up to her car she was wearing nothing but a T-shirt and a pair of flimsy panties. I looked into her lap and I could see right through her panties, and I'm thinking, "Oh shit." But I held it together, and instead of saying what was on my mind I said, "You ever throw me a bird again I'll kick your ass because us country boys don't play that way . . . we'll knock you in the head when you get out of line like that."

She casually looked up at me and smiled and said, "What are you doing tonight?"

I said, "Uh . . . I got work to . . . uh, to do . . . why?"

"Well, do you want to get together?"

I took a step back and tried to think.

She had the most beautiful, innocent looking little face. She raised her eyebrows and with a devilish grin she said, "Well, do ya?"

I said, "Well . . . uh; I don't know . . . uh . . . shit, why not?"

And so, we got together

From that very first kiss, Joey did something to me. I've been with a lot of those girls in the mountains: the single women, married women, their daughters, their cousins, their sisters; it didn't matter. I was with every kind of woman there is in the mountains and I never felt anything like I did when I was with Joey. Something just happened between us, and Joey became my first real love.

I guess you just do things that are stone stupid when you're in love and so I quit riding the pretty girls around when I was hauling whiskey. Joey didn't like me doing that. And so when I hauled whiskey I ran mostly through the hills at night and tried to stay out of town. But, every thing we did was getting tougher to do since Kenneth Seabolt beat out my uncle Ralph Ridley and became the new Sheriff for Lumpkin County. He won the election over my uncle by promising to clean up Dahlonega.

And let me tell you, there was a big fuss over Buford Pusser over in Adamsville, Tennessee when they made that movie, "Walking Tall" . . . but *the real walking tall* was Kenneth Seabolt. He done killed my cousin Snake Martin and Snake didn't play games. He'd blow your head off and just leave you in the woods.

Both these men were dead-up; and Seabolt had no problem taking Snake Martin out.

Seabolt was a State Trooper out of Gainesville and Snake Martin already killed some people. But, one day, Seabolt was told to go bring in Snake Martin. It was just for something petty like making moonshine, or something like that, but Snake Martin said he wasn't going. He stood on his front porch and told Seabolt, "Fuck you, I ain't gonna go nowhere with you and if you step up on my porch you better be ready to die."

Kenneth Seabolt was known for bringing in whoever he went after. When he went to get you . . . you went . . . you either went on the hoof, or you went on the slab, but you went. The rumor has it that . . . . Kenneth Seabolt just shrugged and said, "Ok" and nonchalantly walked straight up on to the porch, and then he pulled out his .357 Magnum and put the gun up against Snake Martins chest and pulled the trigger.

He took Snake Martin straight on out . . . on the slab.

This was Kenneth Seabolt; the man who promised to clean up Dahlonega.

There wasn't a dramatic change that just happened over night, but Kenneth Seabolt was beginning to do what he said he would do, and we were feeling it. All the boys I run with got themselves locked up for boot legging or car thieving and I figured the boys were just getting sloppy and I didn't give it a second thought.

One day, though, I was coming out onto Hwy 9 after cutting through the bone yard (cemetery). I was driving my 62' Pontiac Catalina convertible loaded with moonshine. From the boot leg key to the back of the front seat I had jugs of moonshine that I was hauling to College Park. I had one gallon jugs of liquor in the trunk with a sheet of plywood on top and more jugs on that sheet and a third level of one gallon jugs stacked on top of that one, and I was hauling ass when I ran right past a deputy sheriff's patrol car going in the other direction.

It was Butch, my brother in law, and so I waved and kept on going. He was the deputy caught with that 302 engine and they hadn't charged him with anything yet. We had no idea that would happen. Butch was a lanky 6' 2" and his black hair and dark eyes gave him a sneaky mean look . . . and if a car that he was after didn't stop, he was known for running up and booting their ass off the road. He was good at that.

I looked up into the rear view mirror and saw him whip a u-turn and he raced to catch up with me. My only thought was that he wanted to tell me something or to just shoot the shit. He knew I needed to get to Atlanta and sell this liquor if I was going to be able to pay him this week. I didn't think twice about there being a problem. Even if I wasn't paying him off, well hell, he's my brother-in-law, he never bothered me. He was just a stone cold-blooded crazy son of a bitch, and so we got along just fine.

I pulled over to see what he wanted, "Hey Dawg, what's happening?"

"Hey there, Harold. You on your way to Atlanta?"

"Yeah . . . I'm running late . . . got to go . . . whatcha need?"

"Oh this young fella started with the county last week . . . he's riding with me for awhile. He just wanted to let you know you got a leak in your gas tank."

I got out and walked around to see the right rear panel was soaked, but it wasn't gasoline. I knew that right away. Some jugs had busted when I was coming out of the bone yard, and so I said, "Oh wow, yeah . . . thanks, I'll get that taken care of . . ."

The rookie said, "Pop your trunk . . . let's take a look."

I shot a quick look at Butch and he looked as surprised as I did.

"What?" I said, "Look, I really have to run."

The rookie said, "This vehicle is not safe to be on the road . . . pop the trunk, let's see how bad it is."

Butch said, "Naw . . . this is Harold, man. He's alright."

The way the rookie looked at Butch made me wonder just who was 'the rookie', because my brother in law just shut up. The rookie was looking suspiciously at Butch as he said, "Open the damn trunk" . . . and then he turned his attention toward me and said, "Now."

Now, I was pissed, "I don't have no fucking leak."

"Yeah you do . . . open the trunk."

I thought, if I open that trunk, I'm a caught bitch right here and so I said, "Ok, here's the keys . . . you open the son of a bitch."

I threw the keys way up over his head and when he turned to go get them, I hit the woods . . . I booked it . . . I ran like a son of a bitch.

They didn't get me but they got my liquor, and in the 60's and 70's nobody really cared about catching you. If they didn't catch you at the same time they got your liquor they didn't go looking to try to find you later. The Sheriff got what he really wanted anyway, because very time a car load of liquor was caught, they set the car in front of the jailhouse and the Gainesville newspaper took pictures of the sheriff in front of the car pouring out the liquor.

The sheriff got mileage out of showing that he meant business.

I lost that load of liquor because Joey didn't want me riding around with all those pretty girls. What you give up for love is something else. But I got the feel that it wouldn't have been any different if I was driving through town with all the girls in my car, because this was all Sheriff Seabolt's doings. He's putting new people on the patrols and he's scaring the old ones into doing right.

Maybe my days of hauling whiskey are over, I don't know. Maybe I'm just missing something. Actually, I've been really distracted with things lately because of Joey. When we started dating it was beautiful. But all of a sudden she turned into the exorcist on my ass. I'd be off at work somewhere and she would take my car straight to the North Georgia Ranger camp and lay down with every ranger she met just to make me mad. She didn't go out of her way to hide it, or deny it, either.

But I decided I wasn't going to play her game. I pretended I didn't know what she was all about. And so, we still hung out together. I was giving myself plenty of time to think what I should do about her . . . after all, she may be a cold stone slut but I loved that little bitch.

Joey and I were sitting in my car on the square, one day. We were just talking, minding our own business, when Snooks Brackett looked over and started walking towards my car. He was older than the guys I ran with and I never had anything to do with him, good or bad. All I ever heard about him was bad.

Snooks' had a big round back like a hairy gorilla with long arms. He's 6'3" and weighs 240 pounds. When he fights you, if he can't beat you, he'll cut you, shoot you, or run you over with a car, it doesn't matter to him. He has killed people in fights and just for the fun of it. He's mean and there doesn't need to be any reason for Snooks to fight. If he wants to fight you he will find a way to push you into a fight.

Snooks Brackett came over to my car where my girlfriend Joey and I were sitting. He leaned down to look past me and over at Joey and said, "I want to fuck your girlfriend."

No he didn't.

He wanted to fight, and since he was ten years older than me, and twice my size, he didn't want everybody to think that he was jumping on me. I've seen him around awhile, and I knew that sooner or later he was going to come around and test the waters. Tonight he thought I'd fall for it, "Yeah Anderson . . . I bet she would sure like to have a man for a change."

He thought I needed to try and be a hero in front of my girl and jump out on him, but instead I gave it right back to him. I looked at him and said "I heard you have a woman at home, maybe I'll just go on over there and fuck her."

I touched a nerve, because he jumped back and stood straight up and said, "Well I'll kick your ass if you do." He sounded like a scared little boy.

I surprised him and I saw that he was stunned . . . and so while I had him confused I pressed on and said, "Well, motherfucker . . . you can't do it with your lips, you're going to have to get on me, to kick my ass, and mother fucker, you don't scare me."

That was another thing that shocked him because, here I was seventeen, and he was almost thirty years old, and I was putting it right back on him. He didn't know what to do. He just stood there fumbling for words trying to find what to say. I took advantage of him being stunned for the moment and drove off. I left him standing there looking like the idiot he was.

I knew where he lived and I knew the girl he lived with, and she knew me. I waited for a night that I knew he was going to be away and I went to see her. She must have been as crazy as I was because she let me in, and I stayed all night. Early the next morning when Snooks Brackett came home, there I was, sitting at his breakfast table having breakfast with his girlfriend.

That's just the way I was.

I don't mind taking an ass whipping but I wasn't running and no one's going to threaten me without it getting thrown back in their face. The minute he came in and saw me sitting there at his table with his girl he went berserk. He flew across the room. His girl screamed and I jumped up. I shoved the table between us with one hand and kept my other hand in my pocket. I wanted him to see that I had my hand on my gun or else I was going to have to come out with it right there. But he saw my gun and backed off and so I didn't have to kill the bastard.

It had to be playing heavy on his mind, though, about me, because . . . just how crazy does a person have to be . . . to be waiting for him . . . sitting at his table . . . eating his breakfast . . . after spending the night with his girl . . . in his bed. He knew then that I was a crazy and I wouldn't hesitate to kill his ass.

He said, "Ok . . . go on . . . I'll get you later . . . I'll let you go this time."

I stepped around him as he moved in a small circle and continued to face me. I could tell that he was on the edge of jumping me the second I showed any distraction. To do this to him; is one thing, but to make him take it in front of his girl; is insane, and I loved it. As I made my way towards the door I said, "You ain't letting shit go mother fucker. I'm going . . . I got my shit in my pocket and I got my hand on it . . . you can't get to yours. So, you see motherfucker I'm just leaving . . . and we'll pick this up later."

We crossed paths a few times after this, and he always acted as though he didn't know I was there, but he did, he knew when I was around. He pretended not to see me, but he hasn't forgotten me. He's not letting anything go. He's just waiting for the right time.

I kept putting off dumping Joey. I wouldn't see her for few days and then I'd say, "What the hell," and I'd go pick her up and we'd go off together. But, as soon as we started to see more of each other, she started acting crazy again. Joey tried to make me mad as if she was getting off on hurting me so I would get jealous and fight over her. I still wouldn't play her game. Instead, I started taking her two sisters out . . . her cousins, and then her friends . . . and, one time I almost got her Mama.

Then came the day that I really did have enough of her, and I decided to dump her once and for all. I was tired of just nailing all her family and friends; hell, I could do that anyway. I didn't need to be going with her to do that . . . that was nothing. I decided I would just leave that bitch alone.

But then one day, I ran into her father and he said to me, "I want you to know something, boy, you're not good enough for my daughter . . . I want you to stay away from her . . . I want you to leave my daughter alone."

All the time he was telling me that I was no good, I was thinking to myself, "Ok . . . I got something for you." I was dumping her anyway and he just gave me a good idea. And so, all the while he was talking to me I was thinking, "Well, hell I'll show you who is not good enough".

I went and picked up Joey and we drove from Dahlonega through Cleveland, Georgia and over to Tallulah Falls, and then to Walhalla, South Carolina, and I married the bitch. When we got back to Dahlonega we spread the word that Joey and I eloped and I took my little 63' Ford Falcon and paraded it all over town with a great big sign that read "Just Married — Harold Anderson and Joey King". I did that just to piss off that piece of shit father of hers . . . and when I had enough of rubbing his nose in it, I washed my car, filed for annulment, and never saw that evil bitch again.

Thirteen

Fighting Brackett

Breaking up with Joey was tough, and so was losing my car, and losing all my whiskey, too. I needed to get back out in the woods and make some more whiskey and get back to work and get some money rolling in. I needed to get back to business and cover my losses. And so, I went out in the woods and made some more whiskey and put it in gallon jugs and stashed what I didn't sell. After seven days and seven nights in the woods making moonshine and hauling whiskey I came back into town. I was dog-tired and dirty, but I stopped by a little club we called the speakeasy. It was one of those illegal after hour clubs that didn't have a liquor license and didn't care how old you were, how late you stayed, or how drunk you got.

I meant to come by just to see who was there and if it had a crowd I'd go home and clean up and come back and stay awhile. When I came out of the club I ran dead in the face with that big old burly ugly gorilla, Snooks Brackett. He said, "Come here Anderson, I want to talk to you."

I said, "Look . . . I don't want to fuck with you tonight. I've been in the woods all week long and I feel dirty and nasty . . . I want to go get a bath and come back and enjoy myself. All I want you to do is leave me alone . . . because if you don't, there'll be a killing, and I plan on killing your ass . . . you plan on beating on me but I'm planning on just shooting your crazy ass."

Just then, two old buddies I hadn't seen in a long time hollered over to me, "Hey Harold, what's going on?" They were just going in the club and so I walked in with them and stayed a little while, and then I told them I was going home to clean up and I'd be back.

I added, "That is, if I don't run into Snooks Brackett first."

"You butting heads with Snooks Brackett? We want to see this." My buddies walked out with me, and Snooks knew who they were. They had killed some people, and they were both huge. Snooks wouldn't dare mess with either one of them.

Brackett was arm wresting some fellow and he slammed the guys hand down easily and then called over to me, "Hey Anderson, come on over here o' buddy . . . show me what you got."

I said, "Don't talk to me like we're buddy-buddy, I don't want to arm wrestle with you. I'm going home."

Brackett reared back and laughed, "Hell, you ain't nothing but a punk anyway. You're not strong enough . . . big enough or smart enough . . . you ain't shit, so go on home little boy."

I felt my two buddies watching me and I had all these feelings of being bullied just like when I was growing up. I thought my buddies would be wondering why I didn't do something about this shit that I was taking from Brackett. And so, I walked over to Snooks Bracket, looked him dead in the eye and put my elbow down on the hood of the car and nodded for him to put his hand up, and when he did, I grabbed it and waited.

The mix of the adrenalin right then, and the flashback of people bullying me when I was a boy, worked together for the good because when they said "Go" it was like God grabbed my hand and slammed Brackett's hand down so hard it left impressions of the back of his hand on the hood of that car.

Something was burning in me and so after I slammed his hand down I threw his hand back up in the air, and he said "Oh yeah it's on now." He swung at me and I ducked and all I remember is hitting him one time right between the eyes and I knocked him flat of his ass and before I could even get my senses this bitch turned me a flip right in the middle of the parking lot. My head and the back of my neck hit the ground first. He hit me so hard I just seen . . . hell, I seen stars; and, he just knocked me stupid as 400 Hell. I shook my head several times to get my senses back.

He said, "Yeah get up now mother fucker."

I got up and swung at him and missed, and he hit me again. This time he hit upside my head so hard he broke his wrist but he knocked me stupid as hell. My two buddies got me back up on my feet and I broke loose from them and I ran to my car. I reached in and pulled out my shotgun and I said, "Motherfucker, it's your night tonight" and I pulled back that hammer and was one breath away . . . I'm telling you . . . this mother fucker was dead. But, one of my big old moose buddies grabbed the gun out of my hand and said, "No, Harold; this is not the time" and we left.

I don't know how Snooks Brackett got my shotgun but when I heard he had it, I sent word to him that I wanted it back. You just don't take a man's gun. I let him know if I didn't get it back I was going to come to his house and kill him and his whole family tree. And so, the next day he was riding around the square with a cast up to his

elbow and he was looking at me and grinning and said, "I got your damn gun . . . I'm going to give it back but I broke the firing pin where you can't shoot me."

I told him, "You just don't touch a man's gun, motherfucker, just give it back."

Snooks Brackett looked at me and said, "Ok Anderson . . . you got your gun back but there's one more thing you need to know. This town ain't big enough for both of us . . . one of us got to go."

I said, "Well, good bye then; because I ain't going no where."

Fourteen

Blow 'em away JC

One night I came in on Highway 9 from Dawsonville, and I was alone. I stopped at the all-night station and none of our guys were there. Since the old country man who ran the place didn't like us hanging out there I didn't ask him if any of my buddies have already been by. I decided to just hang out by myself and wait and see who comes in.

Just when I decided to go over to the Square, Snooks Brackett, Doug Walker, and Archie Berry pulled into the station. I couldn't leave now. If I did, it would look like I left because of them. As they drove by I could see the scowl on Archie Berry's face when he saw me. All he had was a little bandage covering the wound to his head where Big Newton shot him with his .32.

They parked on the other side of the station's little office building by the station's Johnny house, and I could see that they were talking and then they would all be looking over at me, and then start talking again, and then Archie Berry pointed over at me, and I felt sure that they were getting ready to jump on me.

Doug Walker climbed out of their car by himself and so I thought maybe nothing bad was going to happen, after all. But, sure enough, he walked straight over and stood right at the edge of the front bumper of my car and yelled, "Get out of that car you little bastard I'm going to kick your ass."

All I could think to say was "Oh shit."

Doug Walker was 6'11" and weighed 340 pounds and I had no idea how someone would whip a mountain like this. I couldn't even believe he was talking to me. What the hell could I do against him?

I don't know what made me do it. Maybe it was because I was scared to death and so maybe I just freaked out, I don't know. I may never know in God's name why, but I jumped out of my car and ran straight at this bastard as hard as I could run and he just stood there laughing. But, when I got close to him I jumped straight up in the air and I just kicked as hard as I could. I wasn't aiming at any particular spot. I had no idea if I was going to kick him in the nuts, the stomach, the head, or if I'd miss him altogether. I just kicked as hard as I could. And here I am weighing a buck 35 maybe a buck 40 jumping on a son of bitch this big. But, I lucked out and my kick got him dead in his nuts and he went to the ground.

As soon as he went to his knees holding his nuts I cut loose and started wailing the hell out of this big old moose's head, and here come the owner of the station with his damn little gun shooting up in the air and yelling, "You fucking little hoodlums . . . you don't cut this shit . . . I'm going to kill all of you." And . . . bam . . . he fires off another shot in the air.

But then, here come my buddy JC. He weighs about a hundred and fifteen pounds . . . and JC is just his nickname . . . he's the one who flipped his Sunbeam convertible six times going eighty miles an hour, and then was too busy laughing about to go get patched up. JC was a character all of his self. He was one of the wildest . . . funniest . . . do some of the craziest shit . . . of any human being I ever saw. Now, old JC was bad about carrying his guns everywhere he went. He always carried two automatic shot guns . . . sawed off and on slings under that old trench coat of his. He's got a new one on today that looks just exactly like the one he tore up in the wreck. People have said he has a closet full of trench coats because I'm telling you, you never see him without it or his shotguns. It doesn't matter what the weather is . . . it can be 90 degree weather and this here cracker's still wearing a trench coat . . . crazy fucking red neck

JC jumped out of his car and yelled over to me, "Hey Harold, you in trouble over there?"

I hollered back, "No . . . I got this mother fucker whooped . . . but the owner's bout to kill us all . . . he's shooting at us out here."

JC said, "Well hell, I'll take care of that son of a bitch." And he come out and threw back his trench coat and grabbed those two automatic shotguns and with about a dozen rounds of double aught buck shot, he tore off the whole top of the building of the all-night station. And, all the while he was firing those shotguns, he was yelling, "My Name is Jesus Christ . . . you can live or you can die, but you're not hurting my buddy to night."

When he finished blowing hunks out of the top of the building he said, "You better get in your car, son . . . we're out of here." Everyone else was scattering like someone threw a rock into a covey of quail. Everyone was running like hell except for Doug Walker, he was doubled over on the ground and he couldn't even stand, forget about running.

Most of the outside lights of the station were shot out and when the noise of the squealing tires, and the shouts of the people died down, the station took on a ghostly look and everything I heard a minute ago seemed to be floating away on the grey clouds that had that sulfur smelled of gunpowder. I sat in my car and through my windshield I saw shattered shards of glass, still in the broken window frame, and pieces of the roof hanging below the ceiling.

I started up my car and caught JC in my headlights. He was standing with his feet wide and firmly planted. His coat flaps pulled back and a sawed-off shotgun in each hand. I just shook my head and stared at JC until he finally threw his coat flaps forward and ran to his car. I was still shaking my head as I followed him through the bone yard. No one stopped us from getting away.

Two weeks after I beat that big 300 pound dummy, Doug Walker, in the ground, Archie Berry comes up to me on the road. He was headed the other direction but he waved me down and I pulled over so that his driver's side was across from mine. He looks over at me and says, "I'm one mother fucker you're not going to whoop like you did your cousin . . . I would have got you that night if that crazy JC didn't show up."

I just stared at him and didn't say a thing . . . I was thinking, now what am I going to do with this fuck. It seems that no matter what I do they just won't leave me alone.

He went on to say, "I should've got your ass that night."

This was puzzling to me. I had to ask, "What? You say you're going to whoop me because I beat up my cousin? What business is it of yours?"

Archie Berry started to open his door, "People who weren't even there are saying you kicked Doug Walker's ass. This shit makes us look bad . . . it didn't happen like that; like the people say it did . . . we didn't get whooped by a punk ass like you."

As his door swung open I said, "Well mother fucker you're not going to whoop nobody today" and I laid my shotgun out the window and pointed it right at him and I asked him, "Now, what you going to do today?"

Archie Berry stared down the barrel of my shotgun and slowly pulled his door shut.

I said, "Ok, let me tell you what you're going to do today . . . you are either going to leave here and never say nothing to me again, or else I'm going to take your head off, right now. What is it going to be?"

He said, "I'm leaving."

Fifteen

The Burning Bush

It was 1972, and there seemed to be a popular movement in the south to crack down on moonshine stills. Moonshine had been tolerated for a long time in the south since it was considered a hobby, and people mostly made it for self consumption rather than for selling. But whether the pressure came from lobbyists for the major distillers or from the government losing too much income (more than half of the retail price on liquor is tax), moonshine liquor had become a major target of law enforcement agencies. The Appalachians are well known for the production of moonshine and Dahlonega, Lumpkin County, Georgia is where the Appalachian Mountain range begins.

When Kenneth Seabolt became Sheriff of Lumpkin County, the handwriting on the wall was telling me that it's time to find something else to do with my life. Kenneth Seabolt was closing all my doors of opportunity. I never was into just straight thieving or robbing. I didn't mind hot wiring a car for parts, or siphon some gas, haul whiskey or make moonshine. But, I wasn't one to walk into a convenience store and get shot robbing it, especially with Sheriff Seabolt on the loose.

The first thing Seabolt did to clean up Dahlonega was bring in the police officer out of Atlanta who ran the fugitive stake-out squad. I forget his name but he was tall and lean with long jet black hair and olive skin. He reminded me of Steven Segal, to look at him, except he had all these mean looking tattoos on his arm. He was just evil looking and just as mean.

The way he operated was to stand behind a see thru mirror and when someone came in to rob the store, he jumped out from behind that window and said, "Trick or treat mother fucker" and blew them away with a 12 gauge shotgun. He was involved in eight robbery attempts and he killed eight would-be robbers, each one the same way.

The City of Atlanta caught a lot of flack because witnesses have said that even when he had the drop on the robber he still said his piece, "trick or treat motherfucker" and then blew him away. He didn't have to shoot them, he just enjoyed the killing. They wanted his ass out of Atlanta and so Kenneth Seabolt brought that crazy son of bitch to Dahlonega.

He wasn't there long and he killed one of my friends. He shot him with a 12 gauge shotgun and one of the pellets went through the eyebrow and into his brain and killed him. And then he castrated another friend of mine with his .357 magnum. He went to shoot my buddy in the back but the little bastard was running through the woods off a stolen car and he went to jump a barbwire fence and, as God is my witness, the bullet went through the crack of his ass and blew his nuts out . . . just took his nuts plumb out.

I never had a problem with him, though, we got along fine. But, I knew he was up there for one reason, and that was to kill us all . . . me, and all my buddies. We got together, though, and we had already planned on taking care of his ass.

But, in this specific period of time, I felt lost. Everything was falling apart. I had these damn ass bullies trying to kill me, and now we're all getting popped by the law every time we turn around. Even when I didn't do anything illegal I was getting in trouble. One night, three of the boys went over toward Cleveland in White county and broke into a store. To this day I don't know their names and I had no idea they were going to do it. But, they came by my place and bummed a ride across town. I didn't know anything about their breaking into any store, but the sheriff knew they did it and he knew they were my buddies, and so he came to my place looking for them. When the sheriff asked me about them I could have lied and said I never saw them but I didn't know about the store being robbed.

So, when the sheriff asked if they were there, I said, "No, they're probably at home."

The sheriff said, "How do you know that?"

I didn't even think why he asked, I just said, "I just gave them a ride home."

Then the sheriff told me what he wanted with them and arrested me right on the spot. I said, "I didn't know they broke into the store and I didn't have a thing to do with it."

It didn't matter to Sheriff Seabolt. He arrested me anyway just because I gave them a ride. And, I wasn't about to give Seabolt any shit, either. They locked me up, and then went out and caught the others and locked them up, too.

They didn't fingerprint or book us. They just gathered us all up and walked us into Seabolt's office. The first words out of my buddies mouth was telling the sheriff that I didn't have anything to do with the break-in, but Seabolt wouldn't listen to them. He said he didn't care one way or the other. He said, "I don't care what you've done or what you haven't done. I just plain don't want any of you around here, any more."

He said, "You boys are getting close . . . mighty close," and he shook his head, "Damn it, don't you know? Some day . . . me, that's right, me . . . I'm going to be the one . . . I'm going to have to come out and shoot your sorry asses. You're not kids anymore, damn it."

I looked at the others and they were older than I was, but I wasn't a kid anymore either, so the sheriff's talk was meant just as much for me as it was for them. Some of what the Sheriff was saying seemed to make sense to me. He was right. I had no direction and no purpose for my life. I stood there thinking this just might be the time to get out of Dahlonega. Hell, I been looking for a good excuse to get out and do something different, anyway.

Then, right on the heels of that thought . . . at the very moment I was thinking of getting out of Dahlonega . . . Sheriff Seabolt looked me dead in the eye, like he was talking just to me, and he said, "I'll tell you what I'm going to do . . . I'm either going to kill every fucking one of you, put you in prison, or you're going to join the Marine Corps."

The minute he said it, and especially the way he put it, I started nodding in agreement and said, "Yeah . . . yeah, that's what I want . . . I want to get out of Dahlonega."

He sent my buddies over to White County where they robbed the store, but he let me go. I had the feeling, all along, that the sheriff was talking to me . . . just to me. It was like religious or something. You know, like when you're sitting in church with a hundred people but, by what the preacher is saying, you know his only purpose that day is to be speaking directly to you.

I heard the sheriff loud and clear, he was saying, "Get the hell out of Dahlonega or I'm going to kill you."

I left Sheriff Seabolt's office with every intention to follow the demands he made, and out of the options he gave us, I felt best about joining the Marine Corps. But, I had no idea how you go about joining the Marine Corps. I didn't even think they would take me since I didn't finish school; but anyway, I figured as long as I stayed away from Seabolt I would be alright.

So I went to Atlanta and that's where I met Karen. We started dating and we ended up moving back to Gainesville and getting a place together. Gainesville was far enough away from Dahlonega, and since it was out of Lumpkin County I would be out of Sheriff Seabolt's hair.

But my work, my family, my social life, my friends, my play; everything I did was either in Dahlonega or some place in Lumpkin county. I realized that without doing anything of what I used to do around Dahlonega I didn't have much else going on. Sheriff Seabolt's options was reason enough to stay away from Lumpkin County and Dahlonega, but something else was bugging me. I knew I was good at something and I wanted to find out what that was. I wanted my life to be more than just getting by, and more than just hanging out. I wanted to change my life in a big way. I just didn't know what that was.

Karen and I took too many trips back into Dahlonega, it was risky, but I wanted to see my friends. I didn't think Kenneth Seabolt was going to shoot me on sight but I didn't want to start hanging out or making moonshine and fall right back into the way things were. The Sheriff was still hot after all my hoodlum buddies, and I already had my warning, so when I went to Dahlonega, most of the time it was just to see my best friend, Danny Brewster.

Karen went with me to see Danny and that turned out to be a bad thing, because Karen went to Dahlonega a lot without me, too. I didn't know about those times until I found out later that she was sneaking back into Dahlonega to see Danny Brewster.

I didn't tell her that I knew about her and Danny because back in those days you took care of business in a different kind of way than you do today, and so I was getting ready to go down there and kill Danny Brewster. But a strange thing happened. Karen was on her way down to be with Danny Brewster and so he sent his wife and two year old daughter on an errand to Gainesville, and a car ran her little Ford Falcon off the road and flipped it. The top smashed her down right on the stick shift and killed her, and it messed up their little girl and put her in the hospital.

That changed my plans for Danny Brewster.

He didn't know that I knew about him and Karen, and so the next day he came by, and he asked me to be one of the pall bearers and I thought, "Ok, this is perfect. His daughter is in the hospital and so I'll have him pick me up and I'll kill his ass on the way to his wife's funeral."

I looked Danny in the eye and nodded OK, but I was thinking "Yes mother fucker I'll be a pall bearer, alright"

On the day of the funeral he picked me up and I had my pistol in my pocket and I was quiet half way to the funeral home and then I said "Look, we got to talk" and I pulled my pistol out and laid it up on my right leg. I said, "I grew up with you Danny . . . you were my best friend but you are a no good dirty stinking son of a bitch . . . I know about you and Karen and I was ready to kill you today on the way to your wife's funeral."

Danny started to say something, "But you don't understand it was just . . ."

"Don't you talk . . . I don't want to hear a fucking thing you say . . . you sent your wife to town so Karen could come down and fuck you, and now your wife is dead and your daughter's in the hospital."

"I'm sorry . . . really man . . . you got to believe me . . . I didn't mean for it to . . ."

"Oh . . . don't worry, I decided not to kill you . . . and the only reason I'm not going to kill you, is because I want you to live knowing . . . that in order for you to fuck your best friend's girl, you sent your wife away to be killed, and you put your own daughter in the hospital. I want you to live with that the rest of your stinking ass life."

And that day, I knew there were three things you can not trust people with . . . that is your life, your money, and your pussy . . . and that has stayed with me to this day.

I didn't let Karen know that I knew about Danny Brewster, either. I didn't know what I was going to do with her. But, I was going to have to do something. I wasn't going to be able to keep it in any longer. I was disgusted with her and I felt utterly and completely lost. And so, one day I was thinking about going back to Dahlonega, even though I knew that would be the wrong thing to do. I was seriously thinking of going back and taking my chances against Seabolt.

I never felt the presence of a 'death wish' in my life more than what I felt right now. A death wish says, *"You're already dead"*. When you have a death wish, what you really wish for is that your death would end. You see; a death wish is not that you want to die; it's only that you wish you would be able to, if you wanted to. It's that you want control of your life back in your own hands, but if, emotionally, there is nothing left of you to die, *"You're already dead"*.

So, if I go back to Dahlonega and fall back in with the same crowd I'll probably get killed, but the way I feel now, I'm already dead. That was what I was thinking as I walked down the street in Gainesville and with each step, these thoughts got heavier, and heavier, until my legs felt as if they were made out of lead.

Something has got to change.

It feels like there's nine million tons on my shoulders and my legs are hurting so bad I can hardly move. As a matter of fact, I stopped right then, and there. I couldn't take another step. I reached the end of my rope because the only thought I had at that time was that I was lost and I didn't know where to turn.

I stood on the sidewalk trying to remember where I was headed and why I was standing there. And then, as clear as day; I heard Sheriff Seabolt in my head, and he was saying, *"I'm going to kill every one of you, put you in prison, or you're going to join the Marine Corps."* I looked to my left and there it was . . . I was mesmerized by a picture of a man in a uniform. It was a billboard and it was calling out to me, it said, "The Marines are looking for a Few Good Men".

It was heaven sent.

Everything that led up to that moment, everything in the last few years and months, and right up to the last second before seeing that sign . . . everything, was telling me that this is a *'burning bush'* and it's telling me, "This is where you need to be, right here, you need to be with us. You haven't accomplished shit . . . you're broke . . . you have no direction in life . . . you have nothing . . . and you are nothing . . . you are absolutely worthless."

I stood there for a long time thinking about what this sign was telling me, and I finally said out loud, "You got it." And I took the address of the recruiting office from the sign and it was like I was reborn . . . somebody took all the weight off my shoulders . . . I knew what I could do . . . I knew how to get out of all this that I was in . . . and it was like somebody just took the lead out of my legs and I, literally, started sprinting.

Sixteen

Never, Never . . . Never Give Up

I was in Gainesville, Georgia and the United States Marine Corps recruiting sign had an address in Dahlonega, twenty one miles away. When I saw that billboard and decided it was for me, I started sprinting and then jogging and in a mile or two down the road I changed it to a walk. I covered that twenty-one miles and I didn't stop until I walked right into the recruiters office in Dahlonega, Georgia, and before saying hi, bye, or what have you, I said, "I saw that sign on the sidewalk that says you're looking for a few good men and I fit that category because I know I'm a good person, and I know I'm a hard worker."

The recruiter stood up from behind his desk and he looked just like the Marine on the sign. He stood straight as a board and there were creases running down his shirt that was creased just as hard as the ones on his dress pants. And damn, his shoes were shinier than any shoe I ever saw. There was something about the way he carried himself that told me I came to the right place.

He shook my hand as he said, "Yes sir, you're the one we're looking for . . . sit over here."

As I took my seat I told him, "Look here . . . I have no education and I'm dumber than a bucket of rocks so what can I do to get into this Marine Corps?

He said, "How old are you son?"

I said, "Well, let's see . . . uh, I'm almost 20."

He said, "Hell, most people join at 17 years old."

I said, "Look here . . . I want to join the Marine Corps. I'm not 17 years old. Can I join?"

"Let's fill out an application" and he grabbed a sheet of paper that had a lot of questions and places to put my responses. I suddenly realized this was not going to be an easy thing to do. But I lucked out because he took that sheet, with all the things to be filled out on it, and he put it in the typewriter, and after he lined it up to suit him he began asking me the questions, "Full name, last name first" and he typed my responses. He continued right on through with the application which would have been hard for me to do, and so because he asked the questions I didn't have to read them, and since he typed in my responses I didn't have to write them, so this part was a breeze.

Then he said, "We got a test for you to take . . . very basic thing . . . simple, nothing to it." He handed me four sheets of paper that were stapled together and pointed to the chair in front of the table across the room from his desk, "You can sit right there . . . no time limit, just take your time, starting now." He got up and left me to do the test.

There were words on there that I didn't know and couldn't read that well so I wasn't sure what some of the questions were asking. And there were some questions that had to do with some basic mathematics and I guessed at those, and there were a few questions on there that I actually think I did pretty good.

All in all, though, the recruiter said I failed.

I was disappointed but I asked him, "So what do I do now to get in the Marine Corps?"

He said, "Well you have to call it a day but if you want . . . you can come back tomorrow and take the test over."

"The same test?"

"Yep, the same test."

I was determined to join the Marine Corps so I told him, "I'll be here."

And I was, I showed up early and I took my time on the test and I was there a long time, but I failed again. But the recruiter said I could come back and take the test over again.

And so I did. But this time I was starting to remember what I got wrong the day before and what the answer should have been, and so I got a few more questions right this time. But even this time I failed the test. It happened the same way the fourth time I took the test; I failed. And when the recruiter told me that I failed after taking the test for the fifth time, I just sat there and felt like shit and I realized I wasn't going to be able to get into the Marine Corps.

I was leaning forward on my forearms, my fists were clenched, and I was looking down at the desk. The recruiter was watching me and we were both quiet for a long moment or two. I was frustrated, and I started spouting off, "Damn my memory, I can't remember shit . . . I can't remember one day to the next . . . and I'm just stone stupid, too. I don't know sic'em from come here." But, I didn't want to give up, and so I stood up and looked the recruiter dead in the eye and said, "Look here . . . I need some help. You need me and I need you and I'll do anything to get into that uniform and be a Marine."

I don't think the recruiter ever had anyone in their office that tried so hard to join, and I guess he never saw anyone refuse to give up, like I did, because he said, "OK son; let's do it again. But this time, don't come back tomorrow. Take this test home and study it for as long as you want and when you know everything on here, then come back . . . and not before."

The recruiter let me take a copy of the test home and I studied it and memorized which ones were the right answers to mark and when I came back the sixth time to take the test, I passed it, and my whole life went into a direction where I knew I could get somewhere. But, before I go anywhere, at all, I have to make a decision about Karen. The recruiter said that the Marine Corps would pay me more money if I was married.

There it was.

Now, I knew what to do with Karen. I thought I ought to get some use out of this bitch and so instead of dumping her, I married her. I never told her that I knew about her and Danny Brewster and I never told her I joined the Marine Corps, either. I just left and never saw her again.

But, the Marine Corps paid me more money because I was a married man.

Seventeen

Semper Fidelis

The kids on the bus weren't kids anymore, but they have yet to learn how to be adults. They were strangers to each other in appearance and mannerisms. They ranged from skinny to fat, city boys to rednecks, some loud and boisterous, others wide-eyed and quiet. They sported every style of haircut from the long shaggy hair to the greased down hoodlum look, and some looked half way squared away because of their short crew cuts and flat tops.

This conglomeration of miss-matched kids had pimply faces, smooth faces, scarred faces and faces that looked lost, worried, excited, and there was even a face or two that looked bored. There seemed to be something of everything one might imagine in such a cross section of kids of this age. There wasn't a thing any one of those boys had in common with the other; outside the superficial. The "cool" ones wore sun glasses, the smart alecks chewed gum, and the boys who have never been away from home over night were trying to camouflage their fear by smoking those little Havana Sweets and talking too fast, too loud, and too often.

It took us six hours and ten minutes to travel the three hundred and forty-two miles, but we made it. The bus came to an abrupt stop at the front Gate of the United States Marine Corps Recruit Depot at Parris Island, South Carolina. A Marine guard walked briskly from his post at the front gate to the bus. He had an aura of authority that appeared to be cleanly cut into each move he made, and even when he was standing still he seemed to have authority over everything in sight. He was a dominant rock of confidence. He stood scanning each seat from the rear to the front of the bus and shook his head back and forth, in disbelief, as he eyed each boy.

Then, he turned to the driver and they shared a smile that we couldn't understand at the time and then he gave a quick nod of his head, stepped smartly from the bus, and took his position back at the gate and waved us through.

The driver was in his early twenties and wore a uniform of khaki colored slacks and matching khaki shirt. He had an insignia sewed on his sleeves that had two stripes with crossed rifles beneath the stripes. On his head he wore a brown hat with a wide brim that went all the way around. The Marine Corps insignia was fixed to the front.

The driver no longer responded to our questions nor did he even acknowledge that he heard a question. His full attention was straight ahead. The steel rigid coldness of the driver was felt for the first time by every boy on the bus.

For the next minute or two we rode in silence through a world in which we obviously did not belong. The bus turned a corner and headed towards an open area where three Marines stood by themselves on a blacktopped pavement that looked to be a gigantic parking lot, but there wasn't a car in sight. They were side by side standing with their feet slightly more than shoulder width a part. Their hands were clasped at the small of their backs with arms bent at the elbows that stuck out to each side. They were dressed like the driver, khaki shirt with creases ironed stiffly down the chest, khaki trousers flawlessly hanging to the tops of the shine on their shoes.

Each one of them wore a hat like the driver wore. It was brown with a wide brim, resembling the hat that was worn by Smokey the Bear. The side of the bus that the door was on faced the three Marines; and then, in one final step on the brakes, the world, as we once knew it, came to a halt. The door flew open and the driver raced off the bus and yelled "Sergeant Quinn; here's your load of maggots" and then he turned and joined the row of others standing there.

These were the Drill Instructors.

Sergeant Quinn was the wiry, hatchet faced Marine who stepped forward and half heartedly yelled, "Ok . . . everyone get off the bus and line up." There was a dash of dry humor in the nonchalant lackadaisical way Sergeant Quinn made his request. All of us on the bus were slowly getting out of our seats, stretching and yawning, and milling around looking for whatever we brought on the bus with us.

Our sluggish movement was exactly the undisciplined lazy behavior the Drill Instructors expected.

Then, as if right on cue, and just as it has happened every time with every bus of recruits before this one . . . all hell broke loose. Three Drill Instructors ran on board the bus while Sergeant Quinn stayed outside and yelled, "I said off the bus maggots," and then louder yet he yelled, "What's wrong girls . . . are you on your period? I said move it."

There was a definite cadence that could be taken as a rhythmic beat sounding out Sgt. Quinn's commands, "I said move . . . move . . . move . . . move, what's wrong maggots . . . you miss your mommy already?" The bus was all but empty when a Drill Instructor who was wider than the aisle stood between me and the door of the bus.

The Drill Instructor was built like a refrigerator and he yelled so loud the veins on his neck pressed out from under his skin, "What the *HELL* is wrong with you fruit face, you like me or something . . . you want to get me in the back of the bus with you . . . why aren't you off my bus . . . are you queer for me maggot?"

I thought, "Damn, I've seen some bullies . . . but, here, too?" I grit my teeth and kept my mouth shut.

"What the Hell are you looking at maggot? Are you a maggot . . . or maybe you're a faggot, which is it boy?"

I said, "OK . . . OK . . . I'm getting off . . . so what the hell's the problem?"

One of the Drill Instructor's grabbed me and pulled me towards the door of the bus and the other Drill Instructor kicked me square in the ass and I flew off the bus and belly flopped flat out on the black top.

Sgt. Quinn was telling us, "I want to welcome you all to The United States Marine Corps where you will spend the next thirteen weeks learning what pathetic pieces of shit you are . . . so, listen to me, ladies . . . I hope for your sake you have had a chance to give your hearts to God, because from now on, your ass belongs to me."

Damn if this didn't look exactly like the same bullying horseshit I was trying to get away from in Dahlonega,

Georgia. I couldn't believe what I got myself into. But I learned there was a purpose for the way the Marine Corps treated us and to tell you the truth . . . I wouldn't trade this type of "bullying" for the world.

There was 13 weeks of Boot Camp followed by six weeks in the Advance Infantry Training Regiment after graduating from Boot Camp, and after all this training we were assigned a job, or an MOS, and shipped out. But first we were given our Boot Camp leave and a chance to go home before reporting to our new duty stations.

I wore my uniform home and I will never forget it. Out of seven boys I was the only one that went in the military and my mother was so proud of me because of it. My mother's sister Ruth was always bragging about her two sons being in the military. They were in the army and my aunt Ruth was always bragging on them. I could see the hurt in my mother's eyes when she saw how much pride her sister had in her sons when they came to visit and wore their uniforms. I could see the look on my mother's face as if she wished so much to have a boy doing something in this world that would make her proud.

But, when I joined the Marine Corps, and when I came home in my uniform; well, that just did it for my mother, it made her day. Nothing could have made her happier than that. She told me one time, and it was the only time I can ever remember her saying this, but she said to me, "I just want to tell you . . . I'm proud of you . . . and I love you."

Eighteen

The Shootout

It's early Sunday morning in Dahlonega Georgia.

Everything feels so different to me. So much has changed in these past two years that I've been away. Even though I've been back a month, now, I still feel like a stranger. The things I used to do don't interest me anymore and the people I used to run with well, hell, they need to grow up.

I lost both my mother and my father in these two years that I was away, but I still have brothers and sisters living here, and even though I'm not close to any of them, I thought I'd go over to my sister's house later today.

What the hell . . . why not?

It's Sunday.

I went to a little café on Crown Mountain to get something to eat and then from there I headed over towards Dahlonega Square. It was a pretty day, bright and sunny, and a light cool breeze kept the temperature near perfect. I was driving along enjoying the day and a song came on the radio and it was a country song and so I leaned forward to change the station. But when I heard the words of the song I sat back, and I let it play.

It struck me odd that this song should be playing at a time that I was feeling the way I did. I had an emptiness that I felt deep down in my gut, and I guess it was because of it being Sunday. Maybe that's what it was. Because the way I saw it, everyone else in the world but me, has someplace to go. And then Johnny Cash comes on the radio with this song, "Sunday Morning Coming Down."

I listened a little closer to the words. Not every word in the song was right on the money as to how I was feeling right then, but some of what he said *nailed* me, and that song described exactly how I was feeling at the time:

> *Then I fumbled in my closet through my clothes*
> *And found my cleanest dirty shirt.*
> *Then I washed my face and combed my hair*
> *And stumbled down the stairs to meet the day.*

Now, I'm not a country western fan. I can take it or leave it. Johnny Cash sung a few songs I thought were good. But, this one, it isn't just the words alone. It was the feel of the sadness that comes through, when he sings those words.

> *Then I walked across the street*
> *And caught the Sunday smell of someone frying chicken.*
> *And Lord, it took me back to something that I'd lost*
> *Somewhere, somehow, along the way.*

I parked quite a ways off the road and moved the car seat down and then laid my head back and closed my eyes and I listened to the rest of the song that Johnny Cash was singing.

> *On a Sunday morning sidewalk,*
> *I'm wishing, Lord, that I was stoned.*
> *'Cause there's something in a Sunday*
> *That makes a body feel alone.*
> *And there's nothing short a' dying*
> *That's half as lonesome as the sound*
> *Of the sleeping city sidewalk*
> *And Sunday morning coming down.*

I dozed off and fell asleep.

When I woke up I couldn't remember feeling so rested. I had slept most of the day. It was late in the afternoon and in March it still gets dark early, and even quicker in the mountains because of the woods. I felt the night time coming on and *this* Sunday was almost gone.

The sleep I got today came from much more than just exhaustion. I believe I was destined to be right here, right now, for a specific purpose; and that there was a reason I was to be rested and that reason was so that I would be at my best. I didn't have thoughts like this, at that time. But, now, knowing what was to follow, I believe everything that happened that day was to prepare me for what I was to do that night.

I headed over to my sister's place across town.

Coming from Crown Mountain Drive towards town I had completely forgotten about the guys that hang out on the square and the way things used to be before I went into the Marine Corps. But, as soon as I saw Snooks Brackett, Doug Walker, and Archie Berry milling around with the same bunch that have always hung out on the square, I got the feeling that nothing in Dahlonega has changed. There they were, just like before I left, all the big ass bullies hanging out on the square.

When I turned the corner and started to drive past them they all looked my way, and then Snooks Brackett stepped out in front of my car and started waving for me to pull over to the curb. I got the same feeling I used to have when they used to come around causing trouble. I hadn't seen any of these guys in a couple years now but I thought those days of bullying everyone were gone. Hell, I'm twenty-one years old, now, so *they* got to be in their thirties, and they're still bullying people.

They were acting the same as they always did. But I felt different about all this now. For me, it really isn't the same. I am a lot bigger than I used to be; I weigh 195 and I've been training in boxing and karate and lifting weights. So, when they waved me down, I got a little grin on my face and pulled over.

Snooks Brackett walked right over and grabbed open my door and said, "You might as well just go on and get out because we're going to kick your ass"

And I'm thinking, "You mother-fucker done gone crazy".

I grabbed this big o' stick and just as I did . . . Douglas Walker, who was 6'11" and 340, was trying to get in the back door of my International Van. Archie Berry, who was 6'5" and weighed 250, was trying to pull the door open on the passenger's side.

My old Van was rocking like crazy. I was trying to pull the door from Snooks grip and had to hurry to reach over and lock the other

door. I had my rifle on the back seat but I couldn't get to it. I wouldn't have been able to get my box of bullets, anyway. They were in the glove compartment; and, I was more worried, right then, about them pulling me out of my van.

A horn honked behind me and I looked up in my rear view mirror and saw it was my brother Eugene. He drove up and got out of his car. Snooks and the others stopped what they were doing and stepped back from my van.

Eugene came up on my side and said, "Hey, what's going on?"

I said, "Eugene . . . why don't you and me whip these dudes . . . just beat the fuck out of them."

Eugene took a deep breath and sighed heavily as he let it out, he dropped his chin to his chest, shook his head back and forth, and as if he was aggravated with me he said, "No Harold, no, just go on now . . . just forget about it."

I said "No. This isn't going to end here . . . this has gone too far. Look, these are grown ass men, they shouldn't be doing this."

Eugene stood there shaking his head, "No."

I said, "Look . . . there's two of us and only three of them, let's just go kick the shit out of them."

But that chicken shit motherfucker just stood there, and shook his head. He wouldn't do a thing to help me. I was going to have to fight them by myself. That'd be no problem, even though they did have guns, because I have mine in the back seat. It was covered up so they couldn't see it, but it's there.

I thought the best thing for me to do was to get the hell out of there. I stepped on the gas and spun around past them and they scattered like quail. They thought I was running and so they ran to their car and came after me. The rest of the guys who were milling around stayed there at the square. As far as Eugene goes, I don't know where he went. I didn't see him after that.

I was hoping to get a little further out of town before I let them pull me over but Snooks rammed his car dead in my ass and knocked me sideways, spinning me into the First Federal Savings and Loan parking lot. They pulled into the lot after I did and blocked the only way out. My cousin Doug Walker, that big stupid fuck, was the first one out of the car. I got out and walked around my van and as I got to the rear, there he was, standing in my face, point blank. I said, "I got something for your ass mother Fucker" and I pulled up my gun and just ripped it and I shot that bitch flat dead in the chest. That .30-06 caliber round chunked off pieces of his chest and back, and he laid down.

Snooks Brackett started to raise his arm up, and he always carried a nickel plated 38, so he started to raise up and I said, "I have something for you too mother fucker" and then I fired a round into his ass . . . and now, this is a bolt action and I'm loading one round at a time. But I didn't rush . . . not one bit, and I had no fear. All I had was a great feeling. It was like I was moving in slow motion but everyone, and everything else around me, was at a dead stop. No matter how much time I wanted to take . . . no matter how slow I went, no one was able to move fast enough to get out of my way. I was calm. I was relaxed. And I was a talking to these fuckers as I was a pumping the lead into them, and . . . it . . . felt . . . good.

Anyone who has ever been in a battle like this would know exactly where I'm coming from. It's not like you hear in all these movies when they say, "I was thinking of getting back to my family, or I was thinking about this, or I was thinking about that". Let me tell you, mother fucker, you ain't thinking about shit, but surviving. During the heat of battle you don't think about a fucking thing but dead up killing the son of a bitch in front of you and doing whatever you have to do, to save your ass.

After I put that round into Snooks Brackett I reloaded and turned my attention towards Archie Berry who was in the back seat. He already shot out the back side window trying to kill me and so I yelled at him, "You can't hit nobody mother fucker, and guess what . . . I got one for your ass, too."

All I could see was this spot on the middle of his forehead where my buddy Big Newton, already shot him once, and that didn't kill the stinking bastard. It just busted his skull up, but he still lived. So they put a steel plate where the bullet went into his head and all I could see was that spot in the middle of his forehead, and so I cocked my head a little to the left and thought . . . *yeah, I'll put one right there . . . right between his eyes I'll fix that mother fucker.*

He stuck his head up and peeped up over the back seat and all I could see was his eyeballs and that spot right between his eyes. I was standing in front of the car and so I shot through the windshield and I thought I hit him between the eyes but the bullet hit the top of the damn seat; and then I couldn't see him, so I pumped another round into the car to make sure I got him.

Snooks had already been shot once but I guess he wasn't hit hard enough, because he took off running. I didn't see him take off until he was about 75 to 100 yards away and so I yelled to him, "Come back here mother fucker and take your medicine like a man." I loaded another round and I had a bead on the back of his head because I wanted to see his head explode . . . I always wanted to see what a 30-06 would do to a fuckers head; and so, I got a bead on the back of his head but something told me, "Don't do it. Harold . . . don't do it."

I raised my sights and shot dead over his head and so he ran in behind some bushes. All I could see was his six foot three, two hundred and forty pound shadow standing up behind the bush. It might have been just a split second passing but it seemed much longer than that, because I had plenty of time to think. I thought, here I am, 21 years old . . . not bothering a soul . . . and these were all grown men in their 30's, and each one nearly twice my size, and they just won't stop jumping on me.

It was dusk dark, I had no scope, and Snooks was just a dark hulk standing a hundred yards away behind a bush, but then a small ray of light hit the shadows and I could just barely make out the outline of his left side shirt pocket, and so I said, "OK . . . mother fucker, I have something for you . . . and here it comes."

I put one right through the left pocket and it went right through his heart and he fell down. Now, he already had one bullet in him from before he ran, but even with this one through the heart, when he fell to the ground he was still moving. His hand was moving in a jerky almost uncontrollably flopping motion and so I said, "Fuck it" and I put a round through the pocket on the other side of his chest and that's when his arm fell down, *and I felt good,* knowing he was a dead fuck.

On the walk back to the car I saw my cousin Doug Walker lying on the ground moaning and shit, and so I said, "Well fuck I might as well go ahead and end this bitches life." I loaded another round and calmly walked over to my cousin and pointed my rifle at his head. I looked at this 340 pound man looking up at me from the ground, bleeding like a stuck hog.

I hesitated so I could look him dead in the eye, because I wanted to be sure to see that big fat head explode when I shot it. But, I heard that voice again, "Harold, don't do it" and this time it wasn't just a voice in my head. I looked up and saw a deputy sheriff and he said it again, "Don't do it Harold" but this time I was looking straight at him with a loaded Sniper Rifle in my hand. He was scared to death I was going to shoot him next, but I didn't.

Snooks Brackett was done. My 'thing' with him has been handled. And so, I thought it over for a second, and then I said, "OK . . . no problem". I pulled back the bolt and the unspent 30-06 round that was meant for Doug Walker's fat head, flew out on the ground.

I was satisfied. I did what I had to do; and so, without any prodding from the deputy I placed my rifle on the hood of my van and I walked over and I opened the back door to the police car and I got in.

It said in the paper that the deputy got the drop on me. That mother fucker didn't get the drop on shit . . . he was scared to death I was going to shoot his ass. They didn't get the drop on me . . . they didn't even put any handcuffs on me. Hell, I got in the police car by myself. The truth of the matter was, they didn't arrest me . . . I arrested myself.

Now here I am sitting in the back of the cop car, which incidentally is easy to get into, but the door handles don't work from the inside and I was beginning to think I needed to get out because hordes of people began to gather. All of Dahlonega was in an uproar because I shot their three bad asses, their bullies, their buddies, and some of these people were their relatives.

I had to tell the deputy, "Do you mind taking my ass to jail and locking me up because you got me sitting in this car and I ain't got no gun. All these son of bitches right here, they all got guns . . . so, take me to jail." That's what it took for them to get me out of there and put me in jail. They took me in the back into the maximum security cell and locked me up.

I wasn't in my cell more than 15 minutes and I was sound asleep. I was sleeping like a baby. I laid down and put my head on that pillow thinking, I just might have killed all three of those pieces of shit . . . and . . . *that* . . . felt . . . good.

Nineteen

Jail

I finally felt free.

Just knowing I was rid of those three bullying bastards was like a heavy weight lifted from my shoulders. All of a sudden I felt so relaxed I couldn't keep my eyes open, and so I closed them. I took a deep breath and stretched out across the bunk and as soon as my head hit the pillow I was dead to the world. But, the second the deputy saw me sleeping he started banging on the bars and shouting, "Anderson, wake up. Hey Anderson . . . I said . . . wake up."

I said, "Yeah . . . Ok." And I sat up and, just as abruptly as it started, the yelling stopped. Since I didn't want to wake up all the way, I just sat there with my eyes closed and so when the deputy quit yelling and went back up front. I let myself fall over on my side and lifted my feet up on the bunk and went back to sleep.

As soon as my eyes closed the yelling started again, "Anderson . . . wake up; wake-up Anderson."

I rolled over and put my feet on the ground, "Yeah . . . yeah, Ok . . . Ok. I'm awake, I'm awake" and I stood up. But the deputy that woke me, left again. I stood there awhile waiting but he didn't come back, so I laid back down and this time I tried to keep my eyes open but, I felt so good . . . I was so comfortable, my eyes just shut and I fell back asleep.

"Wake up, Anderson, come on . . . wake up."

This time I jumped up and yelled, "Why the hell you keep waking me up?"

The deputy said, "Well, I'm supposed to . . . you're on a suicide watch."

I said, "A what . . . a suicide watch . . . for what?"

He said, "We don't want you to hurt yourself."

"Hurt myself? Look man, I wasn't hurting myself, I was trying to sleep. Now, leave me alone."

The deputy looked puzzled, "Are you alright?"

I said "Yeah man, I'm ok. All I want you to do is leave me alone and let me go to sleep."

"Well, we never experienced anything like this before. Why do you want to go to sleep?"

I said "Because I feel good. I just want to lie down and go to sleep . . . I'm tired, you know? What do you think I'm going to do . . . hang myself? Shit, I'm not going to hurt myself. That's why I'm in jail, so I don't get hurt, so take your ass back up front and leave me alone."

After that, the deputy let me sleep. I slept three hours and it would have been longer but I woke up to car horns honking, engines racing, and people shouting. I jumped up to see what all the commotion was but I couldn't see anything. I found out that the sheriff pulled Snooks car out in front of the jailhouse and everyone in town wanted to see the car that was in the shootout. A huge crowd gathered outside the jail and the deputy said he hadn't seen anything like it. The cars were bumper to bumper circling the block, and the people were honking their horns and shouting. It sounded like a wild carnival. Everyone wanted to get a look at real bullet holes and blood, and the windows and windshield shot out. The deputy said, "They're loud until they see the car . . . then, they go off as quiet as a funeral procession."

Once in a while you could hear the words being shouted above the horns honking and the shouts of the crowd, "Where is the son of a bitch".

Someone else yelled, "Who was it?"

"Heard it was that . . . ah, that Anderson boy, Harold."

Then, I heard a familiar voice yell, "Fuck you . . . Brackett and the boys had it coming." I couldn't make out who that was, but it was familiar . . . and that's when I knew my people were out there, too. The crowd was getting worked up and was beginning to sound like a full scale riot. The shouting and the horn honking was getting louder by the minute.

Then, all of a sudden, it got quiet. You couldn't hear a thing outside. It was like someone just pulled the plug of the radio out of the wall and the music stopped. A few minutes of silence went by and then the sound started up again, but now the voices were muffled and the talking was much lower and slower and there was no shouting at all. A few more minutes went by and I heard voices and then the door opened to the hallway leading to my cell and I saw three monster State Troopers coming down the hall. A lineman for a professional football team would have looked small up against anyone of these guys. The deputy leading them kept changing his pace slow to fast and then skipping out of the way, it looked as though he was worried that he might get squashed. They were clearly a head taller than the deputy and when they stepped through the doorway they tilted their head forward so their Smoky the Bear hats would fit through the door.

I recognized one of the troopers from the days I ran moonshine but I hadn't seen him since then. His name was Potts and he never dealt me a crooked stick. He was good man. I wasn't sure he was going to remember me but when the deputy pointed towards me and said, "There's the murdering bastard".

Trooper Potts said, "Whoa boy, hold up a minute . . . you're a police officer; you ought to know better. Number one he's not guilty of anything until a court appointed jury says he is, and number two, Mr. Anderson has done something we should've done a long time ago. It was all a matter of time before Brackett and his bunch was going to get what they had coming to them. That's a good boy you got locked up there. Don't let me hear you say that shit again."

They opened my cell and Potts stepped in and said, "Son . . . you Ok?"

"Yes sir, I'm fine."

"Nobody's mistreating you . . . or anything?"

"No sir . . . the deputy kept coming in and waking me up . . . you know, and I told him to leave me alone because I wanted to go to sleep . . . because, you know . . . I was tired."

Trooper Potts said, "It'll be alright now. Come with me we got to fingerprint you and ask you some questions."

I shrugged and shook my head, "Got no problem with that."

We went up front where they fingerprinted me and took my mug shot and then we all sat down while Potts asked me some questions. The deputies were still in shock that I wasn't in a panic for having shot these three fucks. I was calm and relaxed and when I was giving my statement to the troopers, and they loved it. They asked me what happened more just out of curiosity and because they were interested in the how I did what I did, without even getting shot once, or killed myself.

One of the troopers laughed, "This is some crazy shit," and said, "Damn, you shot chunks out of him the size of your fist . . . he was shot to hell."

One of the other troopers spoke up, "Come on man . . . do you mean to say all you had was a single shot sniper rifle?"

It was more like talking with a bunch of buddies than like being interrogated, but it all wound down and it was time to go back in the cell. The deputy said, "Come on Harold, we'll put you in with the others now . . . no need to have you in isolation."

"No sir, just put my ass back in maximum security."

"No . . . you can go in with the others."

"No . . . you don't understand. I don't want to be in with the others. I'm quiet. I don't like to talk much . . . I like to just be left alone. Don't be putting me in population."

The State Troopers were on their way out the door but they stopped to listen to me and the deputy talking. The deputy got mad, "Look here . . . we'll put you where we . . ." he looked over at the troopers standing in the doorway watching us, and immediately he changed his tone, "Look; I'm just trying to . . ." he shrugged, "Oh well, if that's what you want." Potts nodded to me and the troopers turned and left. The deputy took me back to maximum security.

I stayed two days in maximum security in Dahlonega and when Sheriff Kenneth Seabolt saw that the troopers wasn't coming back he had me moved from maximum security up to the front of the jail. I had a window in full view of the street. Brackett's car was on the other side of the wall from where I sat in my cell. Not only could I see it from my cell, but anyone could see me from the street if I was anywhere near the window. People would be walking around the car but they would be looking up in my direction and sometimes they would be pointing towards my window. Sometimes at night, I would hear a noise outside the window and then a kid's voice, "Pssst, hey . . . Mr. Harold Anderson, sir . . . you in there?" Then I'd hear, "He ain't in there . . . c'mon . . . let's get out of here."

Anyone, who wanted to, could get close enough to shoot me.

One week after I was moved to that cell up front two of Brackett's buddies and his brother were caught in broad daylight sneaking up to my window. They said they were just having fun and all they wanted to do was to scare me. But each one of them was armed and I know sure as hell it was Kenneth Seabolt who set this up. There just wasn't any other reason to move me to the front of the jail.

After the word got out that the Brackett's tried to kill me, a crowd gathered in front of the jail just like it did the first night. It looked like a riot was going to break out any minute. I told the deputy that I wanted to make a call and when he let me get to the phone I called the number that Trooper Potts gave me and I found out the state troopers were already on the way.

Three car loads of troopers showed up and came busting in the jail, doors were flying open, the Troopers were yelling and the deputies moved out of the way. The trooper in charge said, "Open that cell."

Kenneth Seabolt's face was bright red. You could tell he was furious, but he knew better than to argue. Still it wasn't in his nature to sit back and be told what to do. He said, "Who said you can . . ."

The trooper yelled again and the room was suddenly over flowing with troopers and then he repeated, "Open that cell door . . . we're taking custody of this prisoner. The paper work is on the way, but we're going, now."

A mean scowl burned across Seabolt's face but he didn't say another word. He looked at me and then nodded at the deputy who had his back up against the wall. The deputy's hand was shaking like hell as he unlocked the cell and then he moved quickly and stood back out of the way. The trooper reached in, put his hand on my shoulder and said, "C'mon Mr. Anderson we'll take it from here."

The huge crowd that gathered earlier sunk back away from the jailhouse and watched the troopers from across the street. With troopers all around me we walked quickly out the front door of the jail house where three squad cars were lined up with engines running and blue lights flashing. They put me in the middle car and sat my ass between two huge state troopers. There was one car of troopers in the front and the other load of troopers was behind and all three cars pulled away from the curb and moved down the road like one unit, each one moving at exactly the same time, and they carried me to Cleveland, Georgia in White County

After two weeks of being in the maximum security facility in White County, State Trooper Potts came by and stopped in to see me in my cell. They pretty much had all the facts they needed about the assassination attempt in Dahlonega but they wanted to hear if I had anything else to add.

Potts asked me, "Mr. Anderson, why did Sheriff Kenneth Seabolt move you to a cell in wide open view knowing that folks would be gunning for you?" Everyone knew the answer to that question. They knew exactly why Seabolt moved me . . . but no one could prove it. Trooper Potts was fully aware that I knew what Seabolt was up to as well as anyone. Therefore, I believe he asked me that question because he wanted to see what my attitude was about the situation because they were planning to move me back to Dahlonega.

Potts said, "We couldn't keep Brackett's brother locked up and we wasn't able to make anything stick with the other men caught outside your window."

I shrugged, "Not a problem . . . they're just punks. They ain't going to hurt nobody."

"And we can't do anything against Sheriff Seabolt for moving you. He said he didn't think you'd be in any danger . . . but we know different, and he knows we know. That's a good thing . . . he feels us watching him . . . and I know Sheriff Seabolt, he's got a temper, you know. But here, over this shit . . . he knows he could have lost his pension and landed his ass in jail. I don't think he'll try anything more."

I said, "I thought he might try something but to tell you the truth I was a little surprised. When Snooks killed that dude who killed his brother, people were saying that Seabolt was easy on Snooks because they were cousins. But, it wasn't because they were cousins. Seabolt was scared to death of Snooks Brackett even as mean as Seabolt is, he was scared . . . and he's just as scared of Archie Berry, too. He's scared of them both and he don't like either one of them."

Potts said, "Well we'll be coming back . . . maybe next week. We're going to take you back over to Dahlonega and . . . well, we just wanted you to know what's up."

I grinned and said, "Ok . . . It's all right with me . . . Just give me my gun up in there and I'll take care of everything."

Trooper Potts laughed and said, "I bet you would son . . . I bet you would." As he walked out he slapped me on the back of the shoulder and said, "We'll be back to get you next week."

On my first day back in Dahlonega I had a visitor.

I had no idea what was really behind the visit, but this man was clearly on my side, and for some reason it was important to him that I knew it. He introduced himself as agent McCracken and said he was with the GBI, the Georgia Bureau of Investigation. All I could figure out was that I must have paid Snooks back for something Snooks did to this man or his family. McCracken never let on to what it was that made me such a hero in his eyes. He didn't go through the regular visiting routine and meet with me up front. He came to the back, the deputy opened my cell, and agent McCracken came in and told the deputy to leave us.

He started out by telling me what a service I've done for Dahlonega and what a good deed it was getting rid of Snooks Brackett. We talked about a lot of things but the conversation always came back to him saying something that gave me the feeling that his main purpose for him being there was to instruct me how to act while I was waiting for trial. It was almost as if he was telling me, "We got it all worked out . . . now don't screw it up by doing something stupid in jail."

He didn't actually say that, but that's what I was hearing.

He said, "You sit here . . . don't give no problems to nobody . . . keep your mouth shut and just wait for your trial. That's all you got to do . . . and I can't say nothing else."

Then, he looked me dead in the eye and said, "Son, if you build a day in prison I will build it for you. Hear me now, because all I got to say before I leave is that you done Dahlonega a good deed, and if you ever build a day in prison . . . I will build it for you."

After he left I sat down and tried to understand what he meant by that. I couldn't figure out how anything I did that was connected to him. But, his visit helped me stay calm and confident because I knew right then I was never going to prison . . . or at least that's what I thought.

It didn't take me long, after being back in Dahlonega, to understand why I didn't pose the same problem as I did before. Things have changed drastically. Brackett's car was gone from the front of the jail, and there were no crowds gathering, Sheriff Seabolt hardly acknowledged that he even knew me, and all the other deputies were so busy I was hardly noticed at all.

The focus was taken off of me because they had locked up the Lingerfelt man for killing two deputies and hiding them in the trunk of his car. They also had a little black girl who killed her husband. The guy who killed two of his brother-in-laws was locked up, and then there was some other guy no one knew much about and he just killed someone no one else knew much about either.

All these people who were locked up for doing all this killing took the attention off me and that was a relief. But the guy who really got the center stage attention was this crazy dude who killed a state trooper and his buddy. And then, he killed a man in Florida and while they were trying to arrest him he shot two more state troopers until they finally shot him in the neck. A State Trooper shot him straight through the mouth with a .44 magnum and it went through his neck and somehow it didn't kill him. So hell, they patched that bitch up and brought his ass in on a stretcher.

So, here I am blending in with all the rest of these folks who were shooting and killing. To be locked up for murder, all of a sudden got to be common thing in Dahlonega, and I guess I'm the one who got the ball rolling.

This little Dahlonega jail is sitting here up in the mountains, a small ass town to start with, and we got six people in here all charged with murder. The odds of all of us being in this little jail at the same time is something else, and so you can imagine the security in this place. It is a "lock-down" from hell. You'd think we were at Riker's Island or Alcatraz because they had us locked down tight. Nearly the entire population of this little bitty jail is made up of prisoners who done killed someone.

I was happy being locked down most of the day. I wanted to stay by myself. After the first two minutes of talking to the others in here it's all a repeat. They just start saying the same stuff all over again. I don't care to talk to them anymore. First, they belly ache and whine and tell you how innocent they are, and then, they start bragging about all that they had really done. I get sick of listening to their shit.

Twenty

Attorney

The story of the killing was all over the papers the morning after the shootout.

For the next two weeks it was big news all through Lumpkin County and all the way to Gainesville, Dawsonville and up into White County. But the shootout has died down and the controversial trial is starting to loom in the distance and is already starting to take the spotlight.

My brother George is my buddy and the only brother I get along with. He knew an attorney right here in Dahlonega who was just starting out. He never had a case this big. The Brackett's, Archie Berry, and Douglas Walker were known all through this area as bullying thugs, murderers, and thieves. The attorney George brought me was more than eager to take my case.

George came to the jail with him, "Mr. Earle this here's my brother Harold, the one you can read about in all the papers. Harold, this is the lawyer I was telling you about . . . he knows a lot of the right people here in Lumpkin County."

He gave me his card when we shook hands, it read, "Mr. Luman Carpenter Earle—*Attorney at Law*" and he sat down across the table from me. He told me about his business but not anything of a track record. He had his membership in the local and state bar associations, but he didn't tell me of any clients charged with murder that he successfully defended. That's alright, though, all I want from an

109

attorney is someone who knows the law. I have my own idea of how I intend to use him and what he knows.

We had another shorter talk, after the first one, and things looked alright to me, and so I told him I'd like to hire him for my defense and that seemed to make him happy. Then, I leaned forward and lowered my voice and said, "Do you know what Luman . . . this is going to be a big thing around here . . . I can just feel it. This case is going to be good for your career."

The next time we met we got right into the particulars. I ran it down about the type of people I was against with Brackett, Berry, and Walker. And then, the next few meetings we went over the actual shooting and how the events at the square led up to the encounter at the Savings and Loan. We seemed to be getting a lot done and things were going well for us. But then one day, while I was waiting for Luman to show up for a scheduled meeting I started to doze off.

The deputy came back to my cell, "Hey Anderson, just thought you ought to know . . . that is really some attorney you picked. Whose side is he on, anyway?"

I jumped up, "Why . . . what's up?"

"He was in the Court House this morning and was getting up in Seabolt's face . . . literally getting in his face, and Seabolt smelled liquor. Your attorney came to court this morning drunk. Man, that's about some stupid shit"

"What happened?'

. "Sheriff Seabolt arrested his ass . . . I think he called it . . . for . . . uh, obstruction of justice or some shit like that. Man, you better straighten out your attorney. Seabolt's one person he don't want to piss off."

I shook my head and hit the wall with my fist and then sat down on the bunk. I had to do something to keep this stupid idiot from killing me with this case. All I could do right now was to lie back and wait for the bastard to get himself out of jail. I placed a couple calls to George and I told him, "Try and reach Luman and tell him . . . the minute he's cut loose to come straight here and see me. I will not mess with this dumb fuck."

It took the better part of a day and a half but Luman posted his bond and came to see me. As soon as he walked in he was ranting about sheriff Seabolt, he said, "That was absolutely malicious. The sheriff had no cause to arrest me just because I had beer on my breath . . .

and *that* was from a drink I had at four in the morning trying to get to sleep after working all night."

I just listened . . .

"I'm telling you the truth. Harold . . . my alcohol level was no way *near* being drunk. They took it right away but they didn't tell me the results until 24 hours later . . . they made me sit in the drunk-tank all day and all night . . . that's harassment . . . something's going on here that's not right . . . I can feel it."

He quit talking and the room we were sitting in was death quiet. I was leaning forward with my elbows on the table the whole time. I waited another few seconds in the silence and then said, "So you think Sheriff Seabolt was what . . . unfair?"

"Damn right Harold . . . you have no idea what . . ."

"Shut the fuck up."

Luman Earle sat straight up . . . like someone just poured ice water down his back. "Look here Harold . . . if I'm going to take your case . . ."

"Listen to me, Luman . . . just shut your fucking mouth . . . I've been listening to you all this time, now you shut up and listen to me."

Mr. Earle's shoulders sank back down and he cocked his head to one side and tilted it back just a little. And then, he folded his arms and he sat there . . . with his mouth shut.

"So Mr. Earle . . . Luman . . . how much do you really know about the Brackett's?"

He shrugged his shoulders and didn't say anything.

"Do you know much about the family?"

Luman reached down and pulled out a folder, opened it up and turned a few pages and in a soft voice he said, "Let me see . . . it looks like Herman Brackett . . . and his brother, both, have been picked up for everything from being drunk and disorderly to federal charges of explosives and automatic weapons. Yeah . . . I see . . . I understand it's a rough bunch, but I . . ."

I lifted my hand up to stop him from going on. I said, "Wait."

He dropped the folder on the table and leaned back. He folded his arms, cocked his head, but most importantly he stopped talking again, and he listened. I said, "Let me ask you; what do you know about Pauline Brackett?"

He quickly looked down at the folder in front of him like he was going to pick it up, but I said, "No . . . it's not in there."

"Let me tell you. But, before I tell you about Pauline Brackett, go back to the night of the shooting. Do you remember Sheriff Seabolt say that he saw the shooting? Do you remember what the paper said was his excuse for not doing anything to stop these three bullies who were getting ready to put me in the ground? Let me see . . . this public servant, who took an oath to serve and protect . . . he is watching me almost get killed . . . and he said, 'I couldn't go to the scene because I didn't have my shoes on'. That was in the fucking paper. But when he saw Walker go down and Brackett get shot and the whole damn battle turn around in my favor, he came a running."

Luman got a puzzled look on his face and said, "So . . . what are you saying?"

"Ok . . . now, let's go back to Pauline Brackett. Her full name is Pauline Brackett Seabolt, she's the sheriff's wife. Therefore, as long as Brackett had the upper hand it was more important for Seabolt to put his shoes on before he needed to stop any killing . . . but the tide turned and I got them instead."

Luman sat there with his mouth open and listened. "You see Mr. Earle . . . there *is* more here than meets the eye. I killed the sheriff's kin and now I'm sitting up here in his jail. No, I don't think that you getting thrown in jail had anything to do with you. They're after me. I'm the one they're trying to sabotage by fucking with you."

"Ok . . . now, I see it. I see what we need . . ." Luman nodded his head and said, " . . . now, here's what I want."

"Now hold on . . . I don't give a fuck what you want. It's my ass in a sling, not yours. So here's what I want."

"Mr. Anderson . . . I'm your attorney."

"No . . . you're not my attorney, mother fucker . . . you're not my attorney unless I say you are . . . and I ain't saying you are unless you shut your fucking mouth."

Luman didn't know what to say. This was the biggest case he ever had and he didn't want to lose it now . . . not before he even got it started . . . so he just shut up.

I waited for a few seconds and the room came to that deathly quiet again. I hadn't realized we both stood up and were on our feet . . . but he gave in and shut up, so I told him to go ahead and sit down. I sat down across the table from him and I leaned forward on my elbows. For emphasis, I tapped my finger on the table between us as I said in a quiet voice, "This place, motherfucker, thinks it has me good as buried. But you just watch . . . and damn it, you do as I say, period . . . and, no more arguing." I waited for him to acknowledge these conditions.

He said, "Ok."

"Good, Ok now . . . I want you to put me on the stand."

Luman blurted out, "Oh no . . . we can't do that."

I just looked at him with a hard stare and he shut his mouth, folded his hands, and leaned forward on the table and listened.

I nodded once and said, "Ok" and then I continued, "When you put me on the stand I want you to ask me the questions that I am going to write for you . . . and if you don't ask me my questions . . . the ones I write for you, I'm going to fire your ass on the spot . . . in front of the whole town . . . that's a bad way to go, I think."

"Ok Mr. Anderson."

"Ok Mr. Earle . . . here's what I want you to do . . . we don't have a trial date yet . . . get one . . . we need to know how much time we have to prepare. Another thing, since it might be quite awhile I need something to read. Bring me," I paused, thought about it and then said, "murder magazines, you know like "Official Detective" and "True Crime" magazines, I want to see how they set things up and how they do what they do, you now . . . their thinking. And get me any documents that we're allowed to have on my case, and . . . any written statements, too . . . of witnesses. Oh yes, get me some Readers Digest . . . they got a lot of murder stories."

When George heard of my preparations for my trial, he was confused. He got the wrong idea about my reading material. On one of his visits he said, "Harold why are you reading all those murder mysteries, anyway?"

"Well, George I'm not just reading them . . . I'm studying them."

"Why . . . the hell, Harold, are you doing that?"

I said, "I'm writing my own defense, George."

George frowned, "Hmm, I don't Harold . . . what's Luman Earle say about it?"

I said, "Come on, George . . . Luman Earle is a fucking idiot. After all this time I been in here, he still doesn't know what the hell's going on. So I got him bringing me these detective stories, criminal books, and lawyer books and stuff."

"You can't learn all about the law and become a lawyer reading detective magazines."

I said, "I don't have to learn how to be a lawyer . . . my lawyer knows the law, I don't need to know what he knows. But my lawyer don't know people and so he has no strategy . . . he doesn't know the people who are on my side . . . he don't even know who's against me. I have people trying to help me that if Luman knew about them he would screw up their efforts without even knowing it. He's already helped people who are trying to hurt me, so I'm going to work up my own strategy and tell Luman what I want done, and he will do it within the technical points of the law, that's what he knows to do."

George said, "Oh, hell . . . I don't know all about that stuff, Harold. I guess you know better than me."

That's my brother George, my buddy.

He got me this stone cold stupid attorney who I thought, at the very beginning, would be a total washout. But, it's been almost eight months now and we're coming down to the wire and we're ready to go to court. We had our ups and downs, Luman and I, but we got along over all, and I'm banking on him to come through and do exactly what I tell him to do in court.

He was good about bringing me my magazines and when I read a story that looked particularly similar to my case, he was helpful in answering some questions I had about the law in those stories. I think these stories are going to help out. After all, where do the magazines get their stories? They get them from real life, and so that's what I was reading, real life. Some of your best minds, when it comes to the law, are found in the man behind bars who studies night and day on how to get out. I wouldn't go as far as say my mind was even close to being like that of an attorney. I would never be able to keep up with an attorney on legal points of the law, but I think I knew my case well enough to have Luman put me on the stand.

He just never did understand that these are country people. It is not just the crowd who are country people, the jury, the judge, the prosecuting attorney, they all are country people and they want to know the people side of things, not just the legal points of a law that are written down in a book. They want to know the right and the wrong that was being done to the people involved; because these people involved are their neighbors . . . they're all country people.

If I was going to go down for the count I was at least going to have my say in court and I mean . . . *my* say . . . not what some attorney says . . . but what I say.

Twenty One

Death Threats

When I woke up this morning I opened my eyes and stared at the ceiling.

I played back every detail of the shootout on Dahlonega square. I felt a surge of energy run through my body and I jumped up off my bunk. Today I go to court. It has been seven months and three weeks to the day since I shot and killed that piece of shit, Snooks Brackett, and today, I get to tell the people why.

A deputy opened my cell and set my breakfast tray down and then reached back out into the hallway and brought back in a cardboard box, "Here's your clothes . . . after you eat, change, and we'll be back to get you." When the deputies returned I was dressed and sitting on the bunk next to the untouched tray of eggs and grits. I was ready to go. When the cell door opened, I stood up.

The deputy handcuffing me said, "Anderson, we might have a situation out here, today. So, you do exactly what we tell you."

A deputy got on each side of me and another one stepped in front and said, "Ok, let's go."

Up until now, I took all the death threats as just a lot of hot air but by the look on these deputies and the noisy mob outside the jail, possibly Brackett's people are going to try to make good their threats. The court house was just across the street from the jail but the crowd was blocking any way of getting there.

As soon as the outside door opened I was blinded by the sun and I had to put my hands up in front of my face to see anything at all. I heard the crowd but I couldn't make out the faces, I couldn't tell my people from Brackett's. There was shouting from Brackett's people and I heard voices yelling encouragement to me. The shoving of the crowd forced the deputies to press up against me and I could feel us began to move sideways and away from the court house. We were being taken over by the crowd and as soon as the deputies saw that they were losing control they quickly pulled me backwards and we made it back into the jail.

"Come on," the deputy held on to my handcuffs and led me back down the hall, "Let's get you back in your cell."

The deputy heading for the front of the jail said, "I'll call the Sheriff and see what he wants us to do . . . there's no way we're going to get across that street."

Brackett's people were open about their intentions about killing me. There was a rumor circulating that Seabolt was going to be "looking the other way" when I'm taken to the court house. But, the crowd was so far out of control the Sheriff couldn't have controlled them even if he wanted to.

I said, "So what are we going to do? I got to be in court . . . I got to get across the street."

The deputy said, "We're checking with the sheriff, Anderson . . . just calm down . . . we'll let you know."

I couldn't see the deputies but the voices I heard were moving down the hall, away from me, and when the huge iron door at the end of the hallway closed, everything was absolutely quiet. There were no more voices, no sounds of any kind; there was just an empty eerie silent feeling.

I stood and waited but no one returned. Then, I sat down on my bunk and leaned my back against the wall. Several hours later I heard the hallway door open and a deputy came in carrying a box. He pulled out a sandwich in a little waxed paper bag, an orange, and a small carton of fruit punch. He reached through the bars and held it out to me

I said, "What's going on? When am I going to court?"

"Hell, I don't know . . . here . . . c'mon, grab this."

I took it all and asked, "Well, what have you heard? Where's the sheriff?"

"Those death threats you've been getting . . . they're messing things up. I doubt you're going to court today. You got a lot of people out there, that . . . hell, I don't know, man."

"I have more of my people out there than Brackett. Get some of my folks to clear them out and get my ass to court."

The deputy shook his head, "I don't have anything to do with that . . . just hang tight, man." And then he took a step towards me and lowered his voice, "There's talk of moving the trial to someplace else . . . you know, some place outside of Dahlonega maybe, I don't know. That's just what I hear."

"I want to talk to the sheriff . . . get Sheriff Seabolt . . . I want to see the sheriff."

The deputy turned to go down the hall, "Your attorney's out there with him now, one of them will probably be back to see you."

It was my lawyer, Luman Earle, who came to see me, "Harold, we're not going to court today. I told the sheriff that I asked the court to have the State Troopers to come back and handle that crowd . . . so we don't end up in a riot. We'll go to court next Monday."

It was unusually quiet all week long . . . so quiet, that I began to doubt that the Troopers were going to come back. The Sunday night before my trial there still was no sign of the Troopers in Dahlonega. But when I woke up the next morning I had heard that the State Troopers came in late the night before, and that they were everywhere. They were in the courthouse, in the jailhouse, and on the street. Their presence in this little town of Dahlonega was absolutely awesome.

There was a larger crowd this week than there was the week before. Besides the State Troopers coming in, more of my people around Lumpkin County showed up because of what happened last week. Snooks Brackett's brothers and cousins numbered no more than fifty. I had hundreds of folks there who were on my side and was ready to execute the first person to come out with a gun.

The guys who came to kill me last week are afraid to do anything, now. I had people from the North Georgia ranger camp, and from the north Georgia College. I had the down-home, old country folks, and the people I had worked for, and they were all packing guns. These are some country-ass mean people. A gun battle is what they live for, they don't care for nothing. A real, no give-a-shit type killing is contagious and when people are spoiling for a down and dirty fight . . . you can feel it, everyone can feel it, it excites you; and that's why you do it . . . because it feels good.

And you can just feel it in the air today.

If any of Brackett's people come out with a gun there will be a mass killing right there on the square, and nobody will be able to stop it, not even the State Troopers. They got in a circle around me and escorted me from the jail house to the court house; the very same distance I couldn't make a week ago. But this time, Brackett's people backed off and we walked straight cross the street from the jailhouse to the courthouse without a problem.

The courthouse was absolutely jammed.

COURTHOUSE – DAHLONEGA SQUARE – 1975

Brackett's people were disappointed because of the troopers being here. The troopers got me into the courthouse and got me seated. The court room was standing-room-only capacity, and it had been, long before the trial started. The halls in the court house were filled with spectators, too. They had to leave just so the rest of the people in the building could do their work. The courthouse was on the square with little or no lawn or pavement to stand on and so hundreds of people overflowed on to the streets and traffic was stopped, in all directions everywhere, any where near Dahlonega.

It was noisy inside the crowded court room until the judges door opened, and the bailiff said, "All rise", and everyone stood. Judge T.C. Riggins entered the court room and took his seat at the bench, and when he did, everyone who had a seat sat down.

Twenty Two

The Trial

There was some preliminary talk between the different officers of the court and the judge that I didn't understand, but I assumed they were just getting this big O' machine ready to roll. There was some rustling of clothes, some grunting, and the heavy breathing of one more spectator entering the court room and squeezing his way to his seat. A few people cleared their throats, a cough from the center of the room, and then an absolutely dead silence fell which was uncharacteristic of such a small room with so many people in it.

Not another thing was heard until the judge, satisfied with whatever papers he was shuffling and placing in little piles on his desk, said, "Proceed."

The prosecuting attorney started things off by addressing the jury and filling them in on what they were supposed to think about me: "Ladies and Gentlemen, today we will show you that Harold Junior Anderson caused the death of Herman Jerry Brackett by shooting him three times with a large caliber rifle. There is a witness who will tell you he saw the shooting . . . we have the rifle belonging to Harold Anderson which is the weapon that killed Mr. Brackett . . . and we have the sworn statement of Harold Anderson, himself, describing how he fired the third and fatal round into Mr. Brackett as the victim was lying wounded and defenseless, and I might add at this point, unarmed, on the ground."

After he explained that I was guilty of first degree murder for killing Snooks Bracket he went on in the same way of talking about me being guilty of aggravated battery against Doug Walker and aggravated assault with a deadly weapon against Archie Berry. He never once mentioned that they were trying to kill me.

He finished his statement by saying, "Your honor, ladies and gentleman of the jury; this is an open and shut case, there's not a whole lot to it. Did Harold Anderson shoot these men and did Harold Anderson kill Snooks Brackett? Yes, he did . . . and don't take my word for it . . . ask Harold Anderson . . . he'll tell you he did. He admitted that he is guilty, and once you see the evidence, you'll have no problem, either . . . in finding Harold Junior Anderson guilty of all charges."

I watched and listened to the prosecuting attorney paint for the jury a detailed picture of me, as a murderer. What bothered me most was that the jury was looking at me all the while the prosecuting attorney was speaking to them, as if they were agreeing with what he was saying.

I got the feeling that the jury was looking at me out of curiosity, of seeing for the first time and close up, a real live murderer. I couldn't understand how the prosecutor was allowed to taint the juror's thinking when that wasn't all the way it was. There was a whole lot more to it than the picture he painted, but by now the jury's minds are heading off in the wrong direction.

I didn't think to have any opening statements prepared for Luman. All I had were the questions he was supposed to ask me when I take the stand and so the opening statement was all up to him.

He didn't elaborate on anything the prosecutor said about me but he gave what might be considered a respectable beginning. He merely said, "Ladies and gentlemen of the jury, we have no intention to argue that this young ex-Marine, Harold Anderson, is not the same man who defended himself against three would-be assailants the night Mr. Brackett lost his life. Not once has this young man tried to hide that fact."

And, then he sat down, and I was thinking that his statement was a bit short yet I don't believe he has done me any damage. But on the other hand, I doubt anyone's mind on the jury was changed about me being a murderer, either.

The judge turned to the prosecutor and said, "Present your first witness".

The prosecutor did exactly what he said he would do. He introduced four witnesses who said they saw me aim and fire the weapon that killed Herman Brackett. One of those witnesses was the Sheriff and one was the deputy who supposedly "arrested" me. The other two were Archie Berry and Doug Walker. The ballistics report showed proof that the weapon with which I was arrested was the actual weapon that killed Snooks Brackett. Forensics testified that the powder residue on my hands subsequent to the arrest, and the finger prints found on the weapon, proved that I was the one holding the weapon at the time it was fired.

The prosecutor was doing his job. Although it sounded bad he wasn't being overly hard on me. These were just facts that he had to bring forward because these are the facts everyone already knows, and they would wonder why he didn't bring them out, if he didn't. But even with him pointing at me, and making these damaging statements of fact to the jury, something about this prosecuting attorney reminded me of agent McCracken.

It wasn't about what GBI McCracken said, as much as what I thought McCracken might be doing. For some reason he was pretty confident about what was going to happen to me. When he told me, "If you build one day in prison, I'll build it for you" he was sure of something, and, as I watch this prosecuting attorney I'm beginning to understand just what that was.

The prosecutor is stating the facts that are already known but he isn't pounding me with anything that I can see. Now, with a look that nearly betrays what I imagine to be his allegiance to me, he picks up a plastic bag with a piece of paper in it and addresses the jury, "This exhibit ladies and gentlemen is Mr. Anderson's own words. It is the sworn statement he gave after his arrest. I'll read it exactly how it's written, and I quote, *'I put one right through the left pocket and it went right through his heart and he fell down. Now, he already had one bullet in him from before he ran, but even with this one through the heart, and lying on the ground, he was still alive. His hand was moving in a jerky almost uncontrollably flopping motion and so I said, "Fuck it" and put another round in the other side of his chest and that's when his arm fell down and . . . I . . . felt . . . good . . . knowing he was a dead fuck.'* This, ladies and gentlemen, is a fitting conclusion that pretty much puts the lid on the story and clearly shows this to be an open and shut case that could result in nothing other than a guilty verdict."

To tell you the truth, if all I had to go on is what I heard this prosecutor say, I would vote myself guilty. But the real world isn't tied up so pretty and perfect like the prosecutor is trying to make it out to be, because Brackett isn't just an ordinary bad guy. Why don't they just ask anybody in this crowd . . . ask the old women, the old men . . . everybody here is on my side because they know and hate Snooks Brackett. He has killed their sons, he beat their daughters. Brackett wasn't just bad, he was mean. Just for fun of it, Snooks Brackett would stand a girl on her head and use a funnel to fill her full of sand.

He was an evil type of mean. All those men I shot were an evil mean. I'm not talking about just shooting three regular punk ass bad guys. I'm talking about three mean people who have been bullying me, and all these other people around here, for years. Instead of painting my ass into a corner why didn't the prosecuting attorney mention any of that?

I started to feel warm.

I felt a sudden rise in temperature that made me warmer than it really was in the room, and I then realized it was these thoughts that were generating the heat. It became apparent to me that I was getting pissed off for having to defend myself for stopping this menace from bullying people.

Inside of me, my emotions were running around in circles after realizing, for the first time, that this might not go the way I thought it would. I considered that stopping Brackett and his bully buddies was the right thing to do. I'm surprised my killing him is questioned, at all.

But, what I'm feeling, now, is that I might lose this case, and knowing that I *could* lose increases the importance I have to put on maintaining my composure. And so, I closed my eyes and pictured Ollie North during the Contra trials. I could see in my head how calm he stayed and I could remember the coolness in which he conducted himself during the trial. He didn't try to lie, he just told it like it was and kept his cool about it. He broke the law, and he knew he would have to answer for it, but he believed what he was doing was right.

North admitted that he had lied to Congress, for which he was later charged. But he defended his actions by stating that he believed in the goal of aiding the Contras whom he saw as freedom fighters. He was indicted on sixteen felony counts and convicted of three charges for which he was subsequently sentenced to three years in prison. But before he "built one day in prison" his sentence was suspended, and then later his conviction was overturned and all charges against him were dismissed

It must have been that he, too, had an Agent McCracken of his own, backing him up with the same promise I was given when I was told, "If you build a day in prison, I will build it for you." North knew in advance he wouldn't build a day in prison. President Reagan fired Oliver North in public but I believe Reagan was North's "agent McCracken". Oliver North must have received a message something like this from President Reagan, "Don't cause any problems, tell it like it is, stay calm and don't lose your cool . . . and, if you build a day in prison I will build it for you."

I took a deep breath and as I let it out slow, a peaceful feeling came over me. It's the same feeling I get when I'm at the lowest point in my life, and someone I don't even know comes out of the blue, and they know exactly what I'm going through, and then they softly touch my arm and say, *"It's going to be alright"* . . . and immediately, I feel better.

Right then, I made myself a commitment to not lose my temper, to never show emotion, and to not change my facial expressions at anything that is said. I will remain absolutely cool, calm, and collected. I can do this because I know something that no one else knows. Something I can't see is working behind the scenes in my favor.

Earlier, I watched my attorney cross examine all their witnesses but he did so very sparingly, after all, everything those witnesses said was the truth and questioning them too much more about it just allows the jury to hear it all over again, and that just reinforces what they already heard. Mr. Earle was anxious to be through with their witnesses, and to start calling ours, but I was anxious for him to be calling me. I gave him a yellow pad with the questions that I wanted him to ask me, nothing more . . . nothing less, and nothing different.

We had no witnesses stating that I didn't pull the trigger. I had no witness saying I had an alibi and was someplace else. We didn't even have anyone to say that they saw Brackett chasing me or slamming his car into mine. We did bring up witness after witness that testified of the hard work I do and that I was fair and honest and everything else; but, we had no witnesses who could say anything about what was going on between me and Brackett and the others on the night I killed Brackett.

There was no one else to call as a witness, except me, and I already said I did it.

All in all, it wasn't looking good. If the trial stopped right now I'd be heading for Dooley or Rutledge prison in the morning. But we had one more witness to call, and that was me. I got up and went to the witness stand and was sworn in and I sat down. And then, I watched in shock, as my attorney started to get out of his seat with a black notebook binder in his hand. It was opened to a pad of white paper with some writing on it. This was not the pad of questions I gave him to ask me. I nearly panicked.

I looked at him and I shook my head, "no", and he got up out of his seat, anyway. He saw me, and he knew that I knew the pad in his hand had a different set of questions than the ones I told him to ask me. I had to make a quick decision and go against my earlier commitment not to show any emotion or to change my facial expression. He started to talk to me, warming up to a question, and by what he was saying I didn't know where the hell he was going with it. But, he wasn't able to talk to me very long without looking at me; so, when he looked up and we locked in on each other, I just grit my teeth and glared at him with a scowl that said, "If you finish asking me that question I am coming off this stage, out of this booth, and right on that head." That is what he should have heard from the look I was giving him because he was fixing to get me convicted of manslaughter, aggravated battery, and murder one.

Evidently, that's what he heard, because he stopped in his tracks half way through a sentence and turned back towards the table. He made a halfway believable play at clearing his throat and then as if he just noticed he had the wrong pad he said, "Oh yes . . . here we are," and picked up the paper with my questions on it.

There was a long pause as he unfolded the well worn sheet of yellow notebook paper and held it at eye level. He stood still for the longest time, just staring at it. No one breathed, not a muscle moved, everyone in the courtroom was absolutely quiet. I couldn't for the life of me, figure what the hell was going to come out of his mouth next.

Most of the people here are for me and they're seeing my chances, of winning this trial, sinking fast. The crowd was waiting to see something far more than what it had already seen. They would gladly bust a cap in any Brackett who would come out with a gun to hurt me, but they can't shoot the jury if they come out with a verdict that would hurt me.

You better believe, they're waiting to hear more than what they've heard so far.

The way I see it . . . the other side is winning.

The score is three to nothing. It's the bottom of the ninth. The bases are loaded and it's two outs and I'm the only one left in the dugout. It's my turn at bat and there'll be nobody coming up to the plate after me. The trial rests, like this bat, on my shoulder. I am the last witness and I already told everyone I did it . . . and so, all I'm thinking right now is, "My attorney better give me the right pitch, this time, or I'm dead."

My attorney, Mr. Earle, finally lowered his hand that was holding the sheet of questions I told him to ask me, and he made a quick turn back towards me and in a slow southern drawl he said, "Well Mr. Anderson . . . this has been quite an ordeal . . . How do you feel today?"

I smiled to see that we were back on track . . . that was my first question he was supposed to ask me. I said, "I guess I'm, Ok."

"Well, that's good. Now, Mr. Anderson, I only have a few questions to ask you."

I nodded, "Ok."

"How old are you?"

I said, "I'm 22."

"How old were you when the incident happened with Mr. Brackett, Mr. Berry, and Mr. Walker?"

I said, "I was 21."

He asked me, "How much do you weigh?"

"About 169 pounds and I'm about 5 foot 9 inches tall."

"Well how big do you think Mr. Brackett was?"

I said, "Mr. Brackett was 6 foot 3 inches and weighed 240 pounds."

He asked me, "How about Mr. Berry?"

I told him, "Archie Berry was 6 foot 5 inches and weighed 250 pounds."

Luman said, "Well, tell us about Mr. Walker."

I said, "Now that man . . . he was huge. He weighed over 340 pounds and he was 6 foot and 11 inches tall."

Luman feigned a look of surprise and with an exaggerated effort in describing the size of these men, he repeated it for the jury's benefit, "Let me see if I have this right, Mr. Anderson, Bracket was 6'3" 240 lbs; Berry was 6'5" 250lbs; and Walker was 6'11" 340 lbs" he shook his head and asked, "Weren't you afraid of these men?"

I said, "Well wouldn't you be? I was 21 and they were all in their 30's and they've been bullying me my whole life."

Mr. Earle said, "Ok, thank you Mr. Anderson . . . no more questions."

It sounded so different than when I wrote those questions on that paper. It was over so quickly. I realized there was a lot more activity in my thinking when I wrote those questions, but just the point blank asking of them, that didn't do what I thought they would do. I had wished, right then, that I had more questions on that paper. I even wished Luman Earle would go against my instructions, and think up some of his own questions, and asked them. If I ever felt that this case was lost, it was right now.

But, then, the Prosecuting Attorney shot up out of his seat and in a loud voice yelled, "Come on Mr. Anderson tell us the truth . . . where is the automatic weapon you were using that night?"

Well, this guy opened a door that threw me right back into the battle.

"I didn't use no automatic weapon . . . if you look at that rifle right there you'll see it is a single bolt action rifle."

The prosecutor said, "Now come on, Mr. Anderson you could not have fired seven rounds from this weapon in the short time you had to do it in . . . it had to have been from an automatic."

"No it wasn't. That, right there . . . is the weapon I used. The Marine Corps trained me to use this weapon to protect myself and that is what I did . . . I used this weapon. You will see I had twenty rounds in my pocket and seven are missing and there are thirteen cartridges left. I loaded them one at a time and used what the Marine Corps taught me to protect my life."

He turned to the jury and said, "With this weapon, right here, you're trying to tell us, you want us to believe . . . that you . . . five foot nine and weighing only one hundred and sixty nine pounds went against these three huge men . . . I just don't know how you did that."

I didn't see it right away, but he was trying to help me. I mistakenly thought he was asking me specifics of how I physically did what I did, so I started explaining, "Well it was just me taking the bullets out of my pocket . . . now, sir, you got my jacket there and you got the bullets . . . . I said there was supposed to be twenty rounds, it was a brand new box and you got seven missing. I fired seven rounds out of twenty . . . six rounds made its mark, one didn't."

He interrupted me, "No . . . no, just wait a minute . . . all I'm saying here Mr. Anderson, is this; if these three men were as mean as you say they were, how were you able to stop them?"

I said, "Well, Sir, to tell you the truth I was terrified and I was fighting for my life."

"Whew . . . Ok," the prosecuting attorney let out a breath and relaxed, dropped his shoulders, and was satisfied that I finally said what he was trying to get me to say. Then he turned to the judge and said, "The prosecution rests your honor . . . no more questions."

Luman Earle surprised me by jumping up and saying, "Redirect your honor?"

The judge said, "Go ahead."

Luman Earle said, "Mr. Anderson, do you think the amount of force you used to stop these men was necessary?"

I said, "They were already out on bond, waiting to go to court for being in possession of illegal hand grenades, rifles, shotguns, and explosives. I don't think my little rifle was excessive force against all that . . . these people told me they were going to kill me . . . they've been beating on me my whole life. It started when I was real young and kept getting worse and then when I was 16 and 17 they about beat my head off and now they said they were going to just flat-ass kill me."

Luman Earle said, "One last thing" and handed me the plastic evidence holder that had my statement in it and he said, "Mr. Anderson, the prosecution entered this into evidence earlier. You were asked to read the highlighted passage describing you shooting Mr. Brackett. They only highlighted a portion of that statement. Please read for the court the rest of that statement."

I read, "I knew if I hadn't of killed him he would have come back and killed me later, I knew that I had to go ahead and kill this piece of shit. I was going to have to kill him, sooner or later, or else he would end up killing me."

Luman walked over to me and took back the statement I just read and he held it up in the air as he asked me the next question. He was addressing me but he kept his eyes on the jury as he spoke, "Now tell me Harold . . . were you afraid this man was going to kill you."

I looked towards the jury and said, "Yes sir, I was terrified."

My attorney turned back to the judge and said, "We rest our case your honor."

Twenty Three

The Verdict

My back was straight as a board as I sat with my forearms on the table in front of me. My hands folded together and I looked straight ahead with no expression on my face. The judge told the jury to adjourn and make their deliberation and as soon as they began to file out, the room behind us became alive with the gradual stirring of the crowd, and in a matter of seconds the court room was all a buzz.

The judge went to his chambers. Some of the spectators stood and turned to go find the nearest rest room. Most everyone else stayed where they were and began debating the weaknesses and the strengths they thought came forth in the case. There was movement all around me but I sat still; and I thought of Lt. Colonel North. I thought of how calm he was and the fact that he didn't try to color coat what he did . . . he just told the world that he did it and stood ready to pay the consequences. He thought he was right in what he did and he stuck to that conviction. He sat through his whole trial as cool and as calm as any man would, who was committed to his principals. And then, when he was made to face up to the decisions that supported his principals, he maintained his integrity.

I felt no different than he did.

And, oh . . . what faith he proved to have in whomever it was who was acting as his "agent McCracken". His faith was honored by his superior who gave his word, if that in fact is what happened for him. I believe Colonel Oliver North buried himself because he trusted a promise that he was given that he wouldn't stay buried. He fell on his sword for someone, and to have that much trust in another human being is honorable. It paid off for him and I sat in that courtroom absolutely still and continued looking straight ahead as I wondered if my blunt honesty was going to pay off for me.

I breathed in a whiff of Aqua Velva just as I felt the hand on my shoulder. The Trooper said, "Harold, we're going in the back . . . c'mon."

I looked up and standing behind me were four state troopers. Behind them was a mob of people most of which were people who wanted to kill me. The people with a specific purpose always work their way to the front of a mob, screaming and glaring at you. When you shoot three people you're going to have a lot of their relatives showing up at court. The people who were trying to get closer to me were hollering things that would get them arrested for terroristic threats, on any other day.

The four troopers surrounded me and one of them said, "Come on son". I was completely hidden in the center of these four monster troopers as they led me into a side room to wait for the jury's decision. A couple of the troopers tried to talk to me. I guess they thought they were going to cheer me up, or put my mind to ease, but I held on to my composure and didn't respond to any joking or frivolous behavior nor did I change my facial expression one bit.

I sat by the window and looked straight ahead. They caught on that this was my game face; and, the contest might be over for a lot of the other players but I was still in the game. They left me alone . . . they understood.

We stayed in that room a surprisingly short period of time before a knock on the door signaled a fresh flight of nerves in my gut. When the trooper answered the door the bailiff stuck his head in and said, "Come on . . . jury's back." The troopers were surprised we were called back so soon. They said it was a good sign.

I said nothing . . . I expressed nothing. If there was one thing anyone could see by looking at me, they would say they saw absolute confidence. I showed no sign of being worried, or of having the least bit of doubt as to the outcome, because I already knew the outcome. As far as I was concerned, I was told the outcome in advance. And as we made our way back into the courtroom, I heard agent McCracken in my head telling it all to me again, "If you have to build one day in prison, I will build it for you."

After everyone was settled back into the courtroom the judge said, "Ladies and gentlemen of the jury, have you reached your verdict?"

A little lady stood up and in a sweet quiet voice said, "Yes, we have your honor." She handed the bailiff a sheet of paper, he handed it to the judge. The judge unfolded it and read it without showing any sign of what the paper said. He handed it back to the bailiff who handed back to the little lady who was going to speak up for this jury.

The judge said, "Will the foreman of the jury please read the verdict."

And, there I stood waiting. An eternity passed as I watched my life, written on a little piece of paper, being passed from one person to the next. I was 22 years old and standing at the very edge of a fate few people will ever face. The next breath of that little lady, as she reads what's written on that little piece of paper, could put me to death.

But that wasn't my thought.

As I stood there, waiting to hear what these country people felt about what I've done, I was just anxious for all the other people in the court room to hear that it is good riddance to Snooks Brackett, Archie Berry, and Doug Walker and all the bullying that goes on around Dahlonega.

The little lady said, "We the jury of Lumpkin County, the State of Georgia versus Harold Junior Anderson, on the charge of first degree Murder . . . not guilty, and on the charge of aggravated battery . . . not guilty, and, on the charge of aggravated assault with a deadly weapon . . . not guilty.

The judge said, "Case dismissed."

My expression never changed from the time this trial started to the time it stopped, and even now that it's over, I showed no emotion. It wasn't that I really knew what the jury's verdict was going to be that made me calm, it was that I felt absolutely right about what I had done . . . no matter what the jury said about it.

The courtroom erupted.

People cheered, slapped each other on the back, and yelled out, "Way to go Harold." There were hundreds of people on my side who were happy with the verdict and that made it easy to spot a Brackett, a Walker, or a Berry. Because, in and around all those people who were smiling at the outcome, was a dark scowl on the face of someone with their hand in their pocket on a gun. But they were afraid to come out with it because my people had their guns too, and there was just too many of us. Remember, these are old country-ass people and both sides are spoiling for a fight, old women, old men, everyone. The troopers won't be able to stop anything once it gets started. The Brackett's bunch still had their forty or fifty but I had hundreds of folks gathered around and my crowd was growing as the word of the verdict got out.

There could be a Brackett gunning for me and standing unnoticed within any group of four or five of my people, and so six state troopers and four deputies got around me and escorted me back to the jail. I was free to go but if I didn't have these troopers here I wouldn't get far before we had a full scale battle. I didn't see any alternative but to stay in jail and so when the sheriff got back to the jail I said, "Listen, Sheriff . . . all I want to do is be left alone. If I leave from here today and . . ." I paused and shook my head, "Now . . . damn it . . . sheriff . . . you know whoever is coming to pick me up has got guns, high powered weapons, and we got lots of ammunition. And I got a lot of people coming to pick me up."

Seabolt said, "I know that Harold . . . that's going to be a problem, for everybody, including you."

"Look here . . . I've been acquitted . . . I just want to go. But sheriff, if I leave this jailhouse right now there will be a killing. These people will follow me and my people will kill every fucking one of them. So what I'd like you to do is to keep me in jail . . . just take my ass back there and lock me up . . . let me sneak out of here early in the morning."

A couple of the State Troopers who were listening to me talking with Sheriff Seabolt said, "Oh no . . . that won't work."

The other trooper said, "That's right . . . we'll just go ahead and escort him."

I said, "Where to . . . where you going to escort me? Look at that crowd out there you can't get a car through that crowd and if you did, where would you take me that there won't be a Brackett waiting? No, I just as soon stay right here and leave in the middle of the night when they're not expecting."

The State Trooper said, "Then we're staying, too. We don't trust anything about the situation you got up here." Then the other State Trooper turned to the Sheriff and said, "And you don't have enough deputies, anyway. We're not going to let this man get hurt . . . we're staying".

The State Troopers knew I already had my application in to be a State Trooper a long time ago, and I already qualified to take the test. That may be why they were on my side, and if so, I really thank God for that. This whole thing will shoot down my chances to ever be a State Trooper, now, but it certainly increased the respect I have for these troopers. They've always treated me with respect. They even told the sheriff, "We're staying because we don't trust you to protect this boy's life. He's 22 years old and you got this mob out here that wants to kill him, and so we're going to stay."

The troopers took me into the back of the jail and put me in a cell by myself. I wanted to get some sleep, so they put me in there and locked my cell for my protection, and I had two State Troopers stay up in the office and two troopers stayed on the outside to make sure that none of Brackett's buddies were coming to kill me.

About four o'clock in the morning the State Troopers came in quietly and woke me up and while everyone else was asleep they snuck me out the back door and put me in a State Trooper's car and took me to meet with Jerry Harris right outside of Dahlonega. He brought my car, my clothes, and a few things I needed and when the troopers were sure I was clear of any danger, they left, and so did I.

I took off from there and went south, and I didn't stop until I reached Miami.

Twenty Four

Epilogue

"Now picture this in your mind . . . there was an old shack right there and at night you could count the chickens running underneath the house through the cracks in the floor and when it was daylight, the light just come through the cracks in the walls . . . I mean this was nothing but a two room wooden shack. This is where we lived, my mother, my daddy and seven brothers and five sisters. We had no running water, no bathroom and just a potbelly stove to cook on and keep us warm. I would walk up here and wait for the school bus barefooted, and frost on the ground, and cold as a bitch. Barefoot and raggedy hand-me-down clothes . . . and I had to get on that bus with all those other kids.

We were just cold blooded country folks . . . you know . . . and I didn't choose to be in this environment, I was born into it . . . and that's why I work so hard now, because every time an obstacle gets in my way I figure out a way to go around it, under it, or over the top of it because I can recollect back on these days of walking up this little dirt road right here, walking up and getting on the bus and being laughed at by these little rich kids and these little uppity fucks . . . that's what drives me to the person I am today . . . that's what keeps me out of prison . . . that's what keeps me from killing people . . . because if I do something like that . . . it's all over . . . the people who laugh at me would be happy . . .

but, the more they make me mad and the angrier I get . . . I take the anger and the hatred I have for these people and turn it into the energy to go build something . . . just to prove them wrong."

Joshua Lee Patton

Go Ahead

Say it like it is

These quotes are from interviews with Joshua Lee Patton.

They've been added unedited because of the direct and honest way by which Joshua expresses his views.

Joshua Lee Patton describes his feelings about certain things he has experienced in life, in much the same way we would describe our feelings about the same experiences; if we were able to simply

. . . say it like it is.

Say it like it is

When I was growing up, I never had a personal relationship with any person

. . . because of the bullying and being treated like shit.

I could never bring myself to get close to any one because I was afraid that, in the end, they would do me like I was done when I was growing up

We all had that done to us . . . I'm not special.

If you never get abused in life . . . well hell, you ain't never going to have no character . . . you're just going to grow up and be a dud.

Say it like it is

*I look at people celebrating
Christmas, Thanksgiving and
Easter and all that stuff but . . . the
way I look at it;*
   *my daddy shot and killed Santa
Claus and we ate the Easter Bunny
so holidays are non existent for me.*
   *I only have a hard time when . . .
well, with thinking of my baby
sister Sylvia . . . the one who was
murdered.*
   I practically raised her.
   *But someone shot her in the
head and killed her.*

Say it like it is

My daddy . . .
You could never figure him out.
We got along super when he
was not drinking but when he
drank he would just beat the shit
out of me
. . . but it was just the alcoholic
self.
My dad was not a mean person.
I learned later in life . . .
that people who drink alcohol
can get a chemical imbalance
that just . . .
it drives them stone crazy.

Say it like it is

I stay in my 3 foot circle.
I don't want you bringing your
problems into my 3 foot circle,
I don't want to hear 'em.
You created your problem . . .
you live in the environment you live
in because you chose to live there.
Don't blame it on somebody else
. . . and then, tell me how bad you
got it.
People create bullshit and then
they want everybody else to hear it.
I say, "Fuck that".
It's your problem . . . you fix it
and get the fuck up out of my face.

Say it like it is

My life wasn't worth a plug nickel.

I was on a death wish.

I never expected to live past 30 . . . never!

I didn't give a shit if I lived . . .

that's why I hurt so many people and that's why I stayed to myself.

I didn't want any friends, . . . because before the day would be out, they'd probably piss me off, and then . . . I'd have to kill the bastards, anyway.

Say it like it is

*If we're in combat you better
believe I'm not carrying your ass if
you're too lazy to build yourself up
so you could carry your own weight
   . . . we'll both get shot . . . so fuck
you . . . I'll leave your ass behind.*

*That's my policy and that's why
I never made friends in the service
because none of them could keep up
with me.*

*But, they wanted me to drop
back and get killed with them . . .
bullshit.*

*They said, "That mother fucker
will leave me in the jungle".*

    All I could say to that is . . .
        "They got that right."

Say it like it is

In school, we did "duck and cover" drills.

That's when the school bell would go off and we would duck under our desks for nuclear fallout drills.

There was the Missile Crisis and the Bay of Pigs. and then there was President Kennedy getting assassinated . . .

I saw the look and the fear on the teacher's faces and on the bus driver's face. That was the first time I saw adults cry.

I was just a kid,
but something came over me
. . . I knew we were not safe.

Say it like it is

*I tried to be close with the
others in my family but they were
too . . . they were, I don't know . . . I
just didn't fit in.*

*I'm just one of those kind of
people that don't fit in anywhere.*

Because frankly . . .

*I don't talk about the drama
shit they talk about.*

*I don't talk about money
problems . . . or bullshit problems . . .
or family problems.*

*I'm just not a dramatized kind
of person.*

Say it like it is

When my daddy was drunk it was like daylight and dark, like, uh . . . Dr. Jekyll and Mr. Hyde.

I was only seven years old and I encountered him being a nice guy and then monster, and then a nice guy and then a monster.

That had more influence on me, about not drinking.

I saw what it did to him and it had such an impression on me when I was a kid.

I was afraid that if I drank I'd become the same person as him.

Say it like it is

We'd take the moonshine out in the country and sell it to bootleggers . . . and they would triple what they paid us for it.

We made the moonshine and we went sold it in gallon jugs to the bootleggers in the mountains who would sell it in quarts and pints.

We were the liquor makers and they were the bootleggers . . .

In the 60's nobody really gived a shit.

People making whiskey and the law men was relatives.

Say it like it is

In the military my philosophy
was this . . .
   If I am going to train and make
myself better than the enemy . . .

   But you're out there drunk and
dragging your sorry ass around . . .
instead of training to make yourself
better than the enemy . . .

   then why should I take a bullet
to help you when there isn't shit
you're going to do for yourself
                    . . . or for me.

Say it like it is

*But hell, for us boys back then,
the closest things we had to getting
laid on a Saturday night was a trip
to the barn. People laugh about it
and joke about it, but it's true, and
so hey, we weren't past going to the
barn, either.*

*My cousins and I would raid
the barns from time to time and I
guess they'd call that 'statutory rape
on a dumb animal'. But what the
hell, it wasn't any worse than one of
them dumb bitches we were trying
to get into bed*

*Because those old country girls . . .
they wore them old flour sack
dresses and flour sack panties; and
hell, we figured we just might as
well go ahead get us a little heifer.*

Say it like it is

From time to time, we . . . the boys I run with . . . we butt heads with each other, too.

But we have honor and respect.

We're not going to steal from our own, and we don't shit where we sleep.

If we tell you we have your back, we do. And if we say we're going to blow your head off, we will.

We stand up and face you man to man and let you know what's going down and . . .

you can count on what we say.

Say it like it is

I never got no attention . . . I tried hard to be good I wanted to learn . . . I guess I was just . . . I was starving for attention and I wanted to do stuff good . . . I wanted to be . . . I wanted to be liked, and it was . . . not in my makeup . . . you know . . . my family; you're poor white trash . . . that's how they look at you when you got twelve kids . . . poor . . . and you go to school raggedy looking and all that stuff and it doesn't matter how good you try to be or, whatever. They just looked at you like you're white trash and that's how these pieces of shit looked at us . . . but my daddy and mother worked . . . we were never on welfare. I don't even know if they had welfare back then . . . but we didn't do no hand outs . . . everybody worked . . . we had our own way of making a living . . . I mean to support 12 kids . . . well, hell . . .

It wasn't no way for a kid to be brought up . . . but hell that was the mountains . . . that was just the hillbilly way of living, I guess, at that time . . .

ADDENDUM

PEOPLE
PLACES
THINGS

People

THE HILLBILLY

The origin of the nickname of "hillbilly" comes from the "Scots-Irish" settlers in the hill-country of Appalachia. They brought their traditional music to the new world and many of their songs dealt with King William. In 1690, when he was the Prince of Orange, he defeated the Stuart family at the Battle of the Boyne in Ireland and from that day on supporters of King William were known as "Orangemen" and "Billy Boys" and their North American counterparts, the ones who settled in the hills of the Appalachia Mountains, were soon referred to as "hillbillies".

All in all, I'd have to say that "hillbillies" are not what the funny papers make them out to be. I've known some hillbillies that can read and some that can write and some that still have teeth. But, I also know some hillbillies that have shotguns, coon dogs, and some who became pretty street-wise in the city, even after starting life out the hard way in the hills.

I know hillbillies who are as honest as the day is long, who work hard just because that's what they're made of, and I know hillbillies who can take a lick and give back all they took, and then some. I know folks who lived in the hills and on farms and in small towns in the country where no one ever thought of locking their doors or of being afraid to go out at night.

These are the folks most closely related to those who formed this country. They are the foundation of everything that's good and decent about America. It's from these early settlers that we have received the bulk of the principals for which we proudly stand, step forward, and risk our necks to protect.

Places

NORTH GEORGIA

The great Appalachian Mountain Range stretches from New England down to the southernmost tip of the Blue Ridge Mountains and the booming little town in Lumpkin County named Licklog. This little town got its name for being the central location where farmers put out blocks of salt for their cattle. Licklog is located about one hundred miles north of the village known, then, as Terminus, Georgia.

This central rail head, Terminus Georgia, later changed its name in honor of Governor Lumpkin's daughter, Martha. It was changed to Marthasville. The name was changed one more time, and today we call this "village" . . . Atlanta, Georgia.

In the early 1800's when the first gold rush in the country played its role in American History, it was in Licklog, Georgia. Because of the vast amounts of gold found in Licklog, Georgia the Cherokee Indians named the town of Licklog, Ta-Lo-Ne-Ga, which is the Cherokee's word for the color yellow. The white mans version of the Cherokee name, Ta-Lo-Ne-Ga, became Dahlonega.

When Harold Junior Anderson was born in 1952 the population of Dahlonega Georgia was just about 1,900 people.

Things

DIRECTION AND PURPOSE

Josh said, "Remember the shootout on Dahlonega Square?"

I looked at Josh and shrugged, "What shootout?"

Josh shook his head, "Damn, Duke I told you about the shootout on the square. Did you already forget?"

"*What* shootout?"

"Dawg . . . where you been?"

Actually, I heard the story a long time ago. It wasn't that I didn't believe the story. There were newspaper clippings and court records and all the documentation that proved the shooting was the way Josh said it was. We've all had problems with people who have drawn down on us. Sometimes there's a shooting, sometimes not. I guess I just didn't pay that much attention to his shootout, when he first told me. I had too much drama of my own going on at the time.

But today, Josh convinced me to go with him from Atlanta to Dahlonega and have lunch at the Smith House on the square, and then go see where he grew up.

Josh said, "You know, I grew up in Dahlonega."

"What year was that?"

"Oh, that was a long time ago. We were all at home at that time."
"All?"

"Yeah, I had seven brothers and five sisters"

"How'd you all get along?"

"We didn't . . . but I didn't have to put up with them too much . . . I lived down the road with my grandmother."

"Oh . . . that was good . . . huh?"

"No . . . that was bad . . . that bitch was as mean as 400 hell. I would run away from her every day and go back home, but daddy would beat me and chase me right back. One time on my way back to grandma's house my daddy got in the car and tried to run me down."

"He wouldn't really run you over . . . would he?"

Josh said, "He damn sure would . . . he'd been drinking; and when daddy was drinking, he was a monster."

"What was wrong with living with your Grandma?"

Josh said, "Man, I hated living with her. I was about six years old and she made me carry the water from the well that was a hundred yards off into the woods . . . I carried two buckets as big as me . . . one in each hand. I carried all the water . . . all day . . . every day . . . for all the clothes to be washed, for the cooking, and even for the baths . . . and I was not to spill one drop."

We came to Dahlonega to look at the actual streets and houses and places Josh mentioned when he told me the story of the shootout. I didn't expect we would run into anyone who would remember a shootout from thirty years ago. I thought we might find some of Josh's family, but we didn't. Then, I thought just seeing the Square where it took place might move me to some deeper feeling about this 'shootout' . . . but that didn't happen either.

It's been said that *'everything happens for a reason'* and when Josh first told me about how he shot these three bullies and killed Snooks Brackett, I was focusing on *'the shootout'* and so, I could never get it to go anywhere; because in and of itself, the shootout had no place to go.

There *was* a reason for the shootout but I was missing it by a mile. I started to think that the shootout on 'the Square' wasn't what I was supposed to dwell on. Being in Dahlonega with Josh gave me the notion that, maybe, the purpose of the 'shootout' was to direct my attention to the real story, and I was beginning to believe the real story was about the man I was eating lunch with . . . Joshua Lee Patton.

When we finished eating Josh said, "Come on . . . I want to show you something."

"I'm with you, Dawg."

Josh drove and searched awhile before saying, "Ok now, we're coming up on where I was raised . . . we're on Wimpy Mill Road right outside Dahlonega and we're looking at where I was born and raised we're about to get there, we should be there in a couple minutes."

After turning around a couple times and then satisfied we were at the right place he pulled into the drive way to a small house. "We're at my grandmother's house now. This is my grandmother's, right here . . . this is where I was practically raised . . . right here, in that little house right there . . . 1959."

After seeing the trouble he had before finally pulling into the driveway of this plain little house, I held on to a good measure of doubt about this whole story.

He went on describing the time he said he lived there, "Back in the . . . remember the rock wall I told you I built up behind there . . . back in the woods . . . we had to carry water from a spring up there in the mountains . . . we had it damned up. I want to . . . I want to knock on the door . . . that's what I want to do. I want to knock on the door. Maybe . . . these people . . . will let me walk on . . ."

We stepped out of his car and into a slight mist of drizzling rain and I was thinking that this is probably the wrong house and we're not going to find a well producing spring water that he built nearly fifty years ago. I doubt we find anything, at all. But Josh is my friend and he's enjoying himself, recalling all these things from his past.

"Boy . . . this takes me back to old memories right here . . . old buddy."

As we walked towards the house, I was still doubtful that we'd find anything that would make this story click; but then . . . Cona Belle Grizzle answered the door. Josh never did meet her and she didn't know him by Josh or Harold. But, I was shocked when she said she knew his folks and they played together when they were kids.

"You all lived down the road there . . . didn't you? All of you."

"Yes . . . we did . . . but I mostly lived here . . . with my grandmother."

"Your place is gone now . . . where'd you all move to?"

Josh said, "Oh . . . they're all gone now, Darling; . . . and my brothers and sisters . . . them, too, I guess. Anyway, I ain't heard from any of them for years."

She moved her head up and down as she listened.

And then Josh said, "Oh yes . . . Cona Belle Grizzle; let me see . . . now darling, I know a *Doc* Grizzle . . . lives out on Rte 3 . . . you any kin to Doc Grizzle?"

"No . . . uh, my husband might be kin to Doc Grizzle . . . you know Rev Grizzle, Ben Grizzle?"

"Yeah, I think . . . wasn't it along the line of . . ."

"How about a Head? I was a Head before a Grizzle. I'm Ken and Beulah Head's daughter. Did you ever know Jack Head?"

"Jack Head . . . no, but my sister was married to Gene Head . . . the one that got killed in a car wreck . . . they lived up on . . ."

"Uh huh . . . no . . . Gene Head . . . that's a different Head."

"Oh" Josh slowly nodded, "I see . . . ah huh" and then in a sudden burst of excitement Josh said, "Now darling . . . tell me . . . is there a well still back up in the woods behind your house."

"Oh yeah . . . looks like someone built it up . . . uh, placed some stones around where the water comes up out of the ground."

"Oh yeah . . . yeah, that was me . . . I did that . . . I built up that old well . . . and I carried water every day for my Grandmother . . . you may know her . . . Mary Anderson."

"Yeah, I knew an Anderson . . . Mary was a small lady . . . part Cherokee, right? And your mother's name was unusual . . . right?"

Josh smiled when he said the name, "Janelle . . . very unusual name . . . very pretty name."

"Oh yeah . . . I know your mother, Janelle. She was married to Henry . . . he was a twin to John."

"Yes ma'm . . . Henry was my father and yes he was . . . he was a twin."

Cona Belle Grizzle said, "Well . . . I'll be . . ."

Josh paused and he said her name real slow, "Cona . . . Belle . . . Grizzle. Now, that's such a pretty name . . . just like my mother's name."

Cona Belle said, "Oh yes . . . Janelle . . . such a pretty name, and unusual, too."

Harold said, "Miss Grizzle . . . would you mind if we walked up in the back and see the old well?"

"Oh, I covered up the old well when we got city water. But, it's still there . . . you're welcome to walk back and take a look . . . and go on and look around if you want."

The hill on the left rose slightly higher than the one on the right but together they made the sides of a dry wash curving off into the woods from the back of Cona Belle's house. As I walked back towards the old well on the same path Josh used as a boy I felt myself slipping back in a time; and all my doubts about the story I was about to write, slipped away, too.

Josh said, "This was the old shit house . . . we called it a Johnny house . . . now it's the pump house and I built the rock wall up here . . ." Josh walked over and looked at a big pile of little rocks and shook his head, "Wow, I thought these rocks were huge . . . you know, big rocks. But come to see . . . they were just little bitty son of a bitches."

I smiled because I saw the story coming together.

Josh said, "God, this brings back memories . . . I can see me now running up and down these trails. I can see Little Josh just running up here at this stream . . . just playing . . . got a bucket of water in each hand . . . hardly big enough to carry them."

We turned to go and Josh said, "Hey . . . let's knock on the door and say goodbye to Cona Belle Grizzle before we go."

I said, "Yeah, Ok, but first, I need to take a leak."

"Well by God, I do too. We'll just get back to back and piss like two horsemen."